Reasoning and Reading

LEVEL 2
by Joanne Carlisle

 eps

Educators Publishing Service, Inc.
Cambridge and Toronto

Educators Publishing Service, Inc.
75 Moulton Street, Cambridge, Massachusetts 02138-1104

Acknowledgments

I would like to express my gratitude to the Indian Mountain School and the Fisher Foundation for their support and assistance in bringing together the ideas and materials that are the basis for these workbooks. In addition, I would like to acknowledge the assistance of specific individuals who in many different ways enabled me to bring the project to completion: Steven Renkert, Peter Carleton, Isabelle Liberman, Miriam Cherkes, Paula McGivern, Cynthia Howe, Jim Heath, Bruce Carlisle, Ben Carlisle, and the willing and responsive students of the Language Arts classes at the Indian Mountain School from 1979 to 1982.

Contents

Unit I — Word Meaning

Introduction 1
Part-Whole Relationships 2
Classification 3
Synonyms 5
Antonyms 6
Synonyms and Antonyms 7
Similarities and Differences 8
Finding Categories 12
Related Words 15
Analogies 17
Finding Different Meanings 23
Words in Context 26
Definition 27
Following Directions 30

Unit II — Sentence Meaning

Introduction 34
Sentence or Not? 35
Main Thought 37
Getting the Point 39
Jumbled Sentences 40
Phrase Reading 42
Word Order 46
Small Words 51
Relationships — Cause 54
Relationships — Time Order 55
Relationships 56
Relationships — Comparison 57
Relationships 58
Relationships — Examples 59
Relationships 60
Key Words and Generalizations 62
Generalizations 63
Same or Different Meaning 68
Following Directions 71

Unit III — Paragraph Structure and Meaning

Introduction 76
Unity 78
Main Idea 80
Topic Sentence 81
Phrasing Topics 84
Signal Words 86
Examples 89
Support for the Main Idea 91
Cause-Effect 95

Time Order 97
Comparison.. 99
Definition 101
Relationships...103
Practice 104
Following Directions 108

Unit IV — Reasoning

Introduction 112
Fact and Opinion 114
Judging Opinions 117
Relevant Information..119
Inference 124
Cause-Effect 130
Syllogisms 135
Problems and Practice 139
Problems and Practice — Using Charts and Diagrams 142
Problems and Practice — Deductive Reasoning 144
Problems and Practice 145
Following Directions 148

Word Meaning

Introduction

The first unit of study in *Reasoning and Reading, Level 2*, focuses on word meanings. The word is a natural starting point for several reasons. First, it is the smallest unit that has meaning in our language. In addition, it is a basic building block in language. The kinds of relationships which exist between words are also found between sentences and paragraphs. If you gain skill in understanding word meanings and relationships, you will understand many concepts that you will use in other areas of study.

You don't learn about words only by looking them up in a dictionary. There are other ways of learning about words, their meanings and relationships. Here are examples of some of these ways.

1. Many words have more than one meaning. The environment in which we find a word influences its meaning. For example, what meaning does "fly" seem to have in each of the pairs of words below?

    plane — fly   mosquito — fly   flee — fly

    _____

2. Relationships between pairs of words vary. It is important to gain skill in understanding and stating such relationships. For each pair of words below, write a short phrase that shows how the two words are related.

    fence — garden   _____

    all — everywhere _____

    ax — razor   _____

3. Learning to categorize or classify words in different ways teaches you to work with words imaginatively. Even words that seem very different can have characteristics in common. Three of the four words listed below have a common characteristic. What is this characteristic? What word does not fit in this same category?

    ring   tire   doughnut   cookie

    _____

4. As you work with words, you'll learn to appreciate the richness of our language. You'll find that many words have more than one definition. For example, can you think of three or more definitions of the word *spring* without looking in a dictionary? If so, write them below.

_____

_____

Part-Whole Relationships

The purpose of this exercise is to give you practice finding relationships between *parts* and *wholes*. Here are some examples:

A. *lead — pencil*
> The *lead* is part of a *pencil*. (Relationship: part to whole)

B. *pencil — pen*
> A *pencil* is a whole; so is a *pen*. (Relationship: whole to whole)

C. *lead — eraser*
> *Lead* is part of a *pencil*; so is the *eraser*. (Relationship: part to part)

Label each of the following pairs of words **part to whole, part to part,** or **whole to whole.**

1. step — stairs

2. needle — pin

3. feather — bill

4. card — spade

5. tennis — Ping-pong

6. calendar — September

7. nest — egg

8. word — sentence

9. sail — anchor

10. blade — ax

11. flea — collar

12. oven — stove

13. heart — lung

14. zoo — circus

15. bacon — pig

16. axle — wheel

17. cab — meter

18. tornado — blizzard

19. guitar — string

20. elevator — revolving door

Classification

Classification is the act of arranging things into the groups to which they belong. In the exercise below you will be classifying things.

Look at the physical activities below. First, make a list of all the activities that use a *ball*. Second, look at the original list again. Make lists of team sports and individual sports. If an activity could be either team or individual, put it in both lists.

field hockey	hiking	tennis	mountain climbing
waterskiing	skiing	horseracing	bowling
riflery	baseball	badminton	skating
football	golf	ice hockey	volley ball
basketball	swimming	soccer	fishing

Sports that Use a Ball

Team Sports   Individual Sports

Classification

1. Sort the following list into two columns — *blunt objects* and *sharp objects*.

wrench	saw	spear
nail	salt shaker	needle
fork	spoon	candlestick
knife	eggbeater	pan
pliers	stool	toothbrush
mallet	pin	broom
pitchfork	scissors	ice pick

Blunt   Sharp

2. Sort the following list into two columns — *natural items* and *man-made items*.

pencil	milk	paper
daisy	bark	bean
coal	watermelon	peanut butter
cotton	thread	necklace
toast	peanut	glass
nylon	diamond	marble
hay	pretzel	fan

Natural   Man-Made

Synonyms

Synonyms are words that have the same or very nearly the same meaning.
Label each pair **S** if the two words can have basically the same meaning; label **D** if their meanings are different.

_____ 1. slim — slight

_____ 2. groove — mound

_____ 3. many — some

_____ 4. shaky — calm

_____ 5. chief — head

_____ 6. couple — pair

_____ 7. close — near

_____ 8. beneath — beyond

_____ 9. some — least

_____ 10. drag — haul

_____ 11. dust — rust

_____ 12. branch — source

_____ 13. silly — foolish

_____ 14. shadow — shade

_____ 15. type — kind

_____ 16. surface — edge

_____ 17. beat — rhythm

_____ 18. neighbor — friend

_____ 19. join — connect

_____ 20. release — leave

Label each pair **S** if the two words can have basically the same meaning; label **D** if their meanings are different.

_____ 1. travel — journey

_____ 2. raise — move

_____ 3. back — rear

_____ 4. refill — complete

_____ 5. accident — injury

_____ 6. lumber — board

_____ 7. misery — sadness

_____ 8. bend — twist

_____ 9. rough — bumpy

_____ 10. create — repair

_____ 11. save — keep

_____ 12. last — remain

_____ 13. safety — protection

_____ 14. glance — stare

_____ 15. powerful — faithful

_____ 16. quick — rapid

_____ 17. real — ideal

_____ 18. beak — bill

_____ 19. rip — tear

_____ 20. forbid — permit

Antonyms

Antonyms are words that have opposite meanings. The antonym of *hate* is *love*. Below is a list of words. In the blank space beside the word, write a word that is opposite in meaning.

1. war — _____

2. black — _____

3. left — _____

4. beneath — _____

5. break — _____

6. healthy — _____

7. easy — _____

8. friendly — _____

9. enter — _____

10. pleasure — _____

11. warm — _____

12. funny — _____

13. sad — _____

14. deep — _____

15. distant — _____

16. quiet — _____

This exercise contains pairs of words. Write **A** on the line if the pair are antonyms.

_____ 1. create — destroy

_____ 2. annoy — bother

_____ 3. wide — narrow

_____ 4. simple — difficult

_____ 5. hollow — deep

_____ 6. rude — mean

_____ 7. save — spend

_____ 8. long — short

_____ 9. slump — slouch

_____ 10. after — before

_____ 11. beside — near

_____ 12. wild — tame

_____ 13. exit — doorway

_____ 14. forget — remember

_____ 15. humble — proud

_____ 16. pat — stroke

_____ 17. always — sometimes

_____ 18. often — seldom

_____ 19. accept — reject

_____ 20. solid — light

Synonyms and Antonyms

This exercise helps you distinguish synonyms and antonyms. It also gives you practice stating the relationship between pairs of words that are neither synonyms nor antonyms. Label each pair of synonyms **S** and each pair of antonyms **A**. For the other pairs, write a phrase or short sentence that shows the relationship between the two words. The first two are done for you as examples.

1. bandage — cut _____ A bandage protects a cut. _____

2. less — fewer _____ S _____

3. chilled — warmed _____

4. kettle — lid _____

5. drain — empty _____

6. king — throne _____

7. bread — sandwich _____

8. frown — smile _____

9. drawer — dresser _____

10. war — death _____

11. buckle — strap _____

12. confuse — mistake _____

13. miner — gold _____

14. mean — kind _____

15. shark — dolphin _____

16. brisk — lively _____

17. long — brief _____

18. canoe — paddle _____

19. fire — ashes _____

20. powerful — weak _____

21. occur — happen _____

22. bacon — pig _____

Similarities and Differences

We find relationships between things by noticing their similarities and differences. The exercise below gives you practice in this skill. List one important characteristic each pair of words has in common, and then one important way in which the two are different.

Example: mitten — glove

    Similarity: Both are worn on hands.

    Difference: A mitten is worn over the fingers together, but a glove has separate sections for each finger.

1. umbrella — raincoat

    similarity: _____

    _____

    difference: _____

    _____

2. apple — banana

    similarity: _____

    _____

    difference: _____

    _____

3. village — city

    similarity: _____

    _____

    difference: _____

    _____

4. newspaper — magazine

    similarity: _____

    _____

    difference: _____

    _____

Similarities and Differences

List one important way in which each pair of words is similar, and then one important way in which the two are different.

1. brook — river

   similarity: _____

   _____

   difference: _____

   _____

2. parrot — pigeon

   similarity: _____

   _____

   difference: _____

   _____

3. cotton — wool

   similarity: _____

   _____

   difference: _____

   _____

4. silent — calm

   similarity: _____

   _____

   difference: _____

   _____

5. brain — computer

   similarity: _____

   _____

difference: _____

_____

6. balloon — basketball

similarity: _____

_____

difference: _____

_____

7. ladder — stairs

similarity: _____

_____

difference: _____

_____

8. smoke — steam

similarity: _____

_____

difference: _____

_____

9. judge — lawyer

similarity: _____

_____

difference: _____

_____

10. fence — wall

similarity: _____

_____

difference: _____

_____

11. moon — star

    similarity: _____

    _____

    difference: _____

    _____

12. harbor — ocean

    similarity: _____

    _____

    difference: _____

    _____

13. anger — annoyance

    similarity: _____

    _____

    difference: _____

    _____

14. growl — bark

    similarity: _____

    _____

    difference: _____

    _____

15. banana — peanut

    similarity: _____

    _____

    difference: _____

    _____

Finding Categories

Finding categories is another way to gain skill in classification. In the exercise below each line contains five words. Four of the five words have something in common. The other word does not have this common factor. Write down the common factor. Then circle the word that does not belong in the group. In some of the problems, you may find more than one way to group four words in one category.

Example:

Problem: lazy, bored, (happy,) sluggish, tired

Answer: All express lack of interest or energy.

1. carrot, radish, tomato, onion, peach

    _____

2. long, far, fast, distant, beyond

    _____

3. salt, pepper, sugar, orange juice, flour

    _____

4. stay, remain, wait, improve, pause

    _____

5. turkey, chicken, fish, goose, duck

    _____

6. telephone, letter, conversation, television, radio

    _____

7. sky, cloud, steam, fog, mist

    _____

8. boss, master, supervisor, partner, teacher

    _____

9. circle, curve, oval, triangle, diamond

    _____

10. think, finish, complete, decide, end

    _____

Finding Categories

Read the five words on each line. Four of them have something in common. The other word does not have this common factor. Write down the common factor. Then underline the word that does not belong in the group.

1. lame, stiff, sore, crippled, slow

   _____

2. heap, pile, plenty, bunch, stack

   _____

3. buddy, companion, friend, neighbor, pal

   _____

4. demand, answer, claim, require, ask for

   _____

5. tall, large, rich, high, great

   _____

6. hate, love, fear, smile, anger

   _____

7. truck, plow, backhoe, bulldozer, crane

   _____

8. heart, diamond, spade, joker, club

   _____

9. fume, smoke, fire, vapor, gas

   _____

10. skateboard, scooter, surfboard, go-cart, bicycle

   _____

Finding Categories

Read the five words on each line. Four of the five words have something in common. The other word does not have this common factor. Write what the common factor is. Then circle the word that does not belong in the group. Can you find *two* ways to categorize the words in #2 or #5?

1. oil, wood, coal, sunlight, rain

   _____

2. Maine, Florida, Vermont, Massachusetts, Oregon

   _____

3. crack, line, hole, split, gouge

   _____

4. pretty, health, handsome, lovely, beautiful

   _____

5. flowers, grass, gravel, sidewalk, rug

   _____

6. Russia, Australia, China, Paris, England

   _____

7. giraffe, zebra, hyena, lion, buffalo

   _____

8. sand, glass, pebble, rock, boulder

   _____

9. wet, dry, damp, cool, soaking

   _____

10. table, stand, desk, counter, sink

   _____

Related Words

Words can be related in a number of different ways. For example, two words may be things which have similar uses. *Fork* and *shovel* have this relationship. They are both used to dig into and pick up things. They also look somewhat alike. We may notice words that are similar in meaning or opposite in meaning, words that mean places and things associated with them, (bakery, bread) or words that mean people and the things they use in their particular jobs or hobbies (carpenter, hammer). The following exercise helps you become aware of some of the many relationships that words have. Read the first word. Then find the word in the row that seems most closely related in meaning. Underline this word. Be ready to explain how each pair of words is related.

1. **rat**	rodent	cat	snake	pest
2. **blade**	club	gun	arrow	knife
3. **sing**	hike	sit	cook	talk
4. **sign**	label	learn	noise	line
5. **flour**	teabag	garlic	powder	cook
6. **lettuce**	sandwich	onion	peach	spinach
7. **group**	books	school	team	package
8. **drain**	empty	spring	fill	mix
9. **scare**	cut	bruise	witch	chase
10. **wood**	marble	paint	nail	tree
11. **pair**	bunch	shoes	shirt	flock
12. **catch**	match	change	crack	trap
13. **goal**	sport	score	store	start
14. **mad**	bad	sad	crazy	lazy
15. **arm**	frame	badge	strap	sleeve
16. **colt**	steer	cat	fawn	cow
17. **alone**	a lot	about	one	once
18. **bug**	bag	bird	bone	boy
19. **box**	fox	fight	shoes	fix
20. **ax**	hammer	wrench	saw	rake

Related Words

Read the first word in each line. Then circle the word in the group that is most closely related to the first word. Be ready to explain how the words are related.

1. **lend**   hand   bend   borrow   break

2. **bowl**   table   fruit   cup   fork

3. **begin**   again   give   end   leave

4. **penny**   candy   handy   spent   cent

5. **hoof**   clank   tail   paw   leg

6. **past**   blast   fast   long   gone

7. **dot**   spot   span   block   black

8. **pole**   board   rod   ring   rope

9. **match**   batch   flame   name   lame

10. **mail**   man   letter   getter   plane

11. **lamb**   goat   cow   sow   sheep

12. **fog**   sky   mist   humid   fly

13. **temple**   steeple   birch   church   thimble

14. **shake**   shook   took   bang   make

15. **tent**   hover   cover   bent   stand

16. **few**   grew   still   many   two

17. **trumpet** bang   metal   horse   horn

18. **duck**   marsh   swim   swan   swipe

19. **candle**   handle   light   bright   table

20. **clip**   staple   simple   stamp   slip

Analogies

When we do analogy problems, we try to discover the way two words are related to each other. Then we look for a second pair of words that has that same relationship. Look at the following example:

Light is to *dark* as *first* is to _____.

First, we need to consider the relationship between *light* and *dark*. We realize that *light* is the opposite of *dark*; the relationship is that of *opposites*. The first word of the second pair has been given to us, so we know we need to find a word that is the opposite of *first*. *Last* is the opposite of *first*; it completes the analogy correctly.

Using this method, complete each analogy below.

1. *Reward* is to *punishment* as *victory* is to _____.

2. *Loyal* is to *faithful* as *sad* is to _____.

3. *Canary* is to *cage* as *fish* is to _____.

4. *Weather* is to *rain* as *vehicle* is to _____.

5. *Banana* is to *bunch* as *goose* is to _____.

6. *Pull* is to *tear* as *drop* is to _____.

7. *Sip* is to *gulp* as *glance* is to _____.

8. *Compass* is to *circle* as *ruler* is to _____.

9. *Flea* is to *dog* as *termite* is to _____.

10. *Courage* is to *cowardice* as *strength* is to _____.

11. *Hand* is to *thumb* as *cup* is to _____.

12. *Energetic* is to *lively* as *difficult* is to _____.

13. *Stove* is to *cook* as *desk* is to _____.

14. *Red* is to *pink* as *black* is to _____.

15. *Rush* is to *delay* as *spend* is to _____.

Complete each analogy below.

1. *Key* is to *door* as *combination* is to _____.

2. *Action* is to *verb* as *thing* is to _____.

3. *Disease* is to *cure* as *rip* is to _____.

4. *Sadness* is to *sorrow* as *happiness* is to _____.

5. *Go* is to *gone* as *break* is to _____.

6. *Square* is to *box* as *circle* is to _____.

7. *Tomorrow* is to *yesterday* as *future* is to _____.

8. *Queen* is to *prince* as *mother* is to _____.

9. *Wealth* is to *poverty* as *success* is to _____.

10. *Sixteen* is to *twelve* as *eleven* is to _____.

11. *Timid* is to *bold* as *quiet* is to _____.

12. *Vessel* is to *captain* as *city* is to _____.

13. *Bay* is to *ocean* as *peninsula* is to _____.

14. *Tap* is to *shove* as *breeze* is to _____.

15. *Pea* is to *pod* as *nut* is to _____.

16. *Roller skate* is to *wheel* as *ice skate* is to _____.

17. *Bagel* is to *baker* as *steak* is to _____.

18. *Almost* is to *nearly* as *all* is to _____.

19. *Mountain* is to *valley* as *convex* is to _____.

20. *Whirlpool* is to *water* as *tornado* is to _____.

Analogies

Circle the word among the four choices that creates the **same relationship** between the second pair of words as you find between the first pair of words. To show that you have read this, underline the first word in the directions.

1. *Sea* is to *coast* as *river* is to
   a. inlet   b. delta   c. stream   d. bank

2. *Hand* is to *elbow* as *foot* is to
   a. muscle   b. knee   c. ankle   d. toe

3. *Pit* is to *peach* as *sun* is to
   a. planet   b. moon   c. orbit   d. solar system

4. *Leather* is to *shoe* as *wool* is to
   a. goose   b. sweater   c. roast   d. calf

5. *Savings* is to *poverty* as *vaccination* is to
   a. disease   b. doctor   c. needle   d. nurse

6. *War* is to *peace* as *drought* is to
   a. food   b. flood   c. calm   d. film

7. *Pat* is to *tap* as *tar* is to
   a. rut   b. cur   c. pit   d. rat

8. *Sand* is to *glass* as *clay* is to
   a. stone   b. hay   c. bricks   d. dirt

9. *Limb* is to *twig* as *blossom* is to
   a. texture   b. leaf   c. plant   d. garden

10. *Create* is to *invent* as *copy* is to
    a. draw   b. confuse   c. imitate   d. begin

11. *Dry* is to *moist* as *shy* is to
    a. lonely   b. friendly   c. difficult   d. joyful

12. *Pattern* is to *model* as *road* is to
    a. vehicle   b. ride   c. travel   d. street

Analogies

Your task in this exercise is to find pairs of words that have very similar relationships to each other. Read the pair of words in italics. Figure out the relationship between these two words. Then find the pair of words below that has the **same relationship**. Circle the letter before this pair of words. Be ready to explain the similar relationship between the two pairs of words.

1. *sand : beach* ::
   a. shell : fish
   b. rock : mountain
   c. valley : stream
   d. tomato : lettuce

2. *eggs : bacon* ::
   a. soup : alphabet
   b. rye : wheat
   c. peanut butter : jelly
   d. baked : fried

3. *boxer : gloves* : :
   a. cook : stove
   b. soccer : field
   c. reader : glasses
   d. cow : milk

4. *please : thank you* ::
   a. hope : help
   b. begin : start
   c. why : where
   d. ask : answer

5. *poison : death* ::
   a. book : wisdom
   b. music : drum
   c. cut : bleeding
   d. life : joy

6. *sweater : warmth* ::
   a. wool : cotton
   b. beauty : lipstick
   c. food : energy
   d. table : eat

7. *water : swimming* ::
   a. egg : boiling
   b. fire : flaming
   c. sport: running
   d. bench : sitting

8. *thin : skinny* : :
   a. repair : paint
   b. timid : shy
   c. push : pull
   d. crush : hug

9. *fruit : orchard* : :
   a. fish : sea
   b. petal : root
   c. mill : lumber
   d. egg : carton

10. *black : gray* : :
    a. boast : toast
    b. tall : wide
    c. boiling : hot
    d. least : most

11. *rake : leaves* ::
    a. typewriter : pencil
    b. basket : peaches
    c. soup : crackers
    d. spoon : soup

12. *tape : tear* ::
    a. bandage : cut
    b. towel : shower
    c. paint : house
    d. sweep : wash

Analogies

Check the letter of the pair of words that has the **same relationship** as the numbered pair of words.

1. *geese : flock* ::
   a. kittens : cat
   b. cards : deck
   c. bunch : grapes
   d. fruit : bowl

2. *fall : pain* ::
   a. fly : walk
   b. hunger : food
   c. laugh : joke
   d. crime : punishment

3. *pedal : bicycle* ::
   a. battery : flashlight
   b. piano : violin
   c. nail : hammer
   d. wagon : wheel

4. *electricity : wire* ::
   a. steam : kettle
   b. gas : fuel
   c. water : hose
   d. engine : oil

5. *absent : present* ::
   a. dangerous : safe
   b. steady : even
   c. confuse : frustrate
   d. horse : stable

6. *pistol : trigger* : :
   a. blade : sword
   b. light : switch
   c. holster : belt
   d. rifle : case

7. *diet : weight* ::
   a. food : fat
   b. dinner : smell
   c. height : inches
   d. drug : pain

8. *like : love* ::
   a. pound : hit
   b. friend : enemy
   c. mad : furious
   d. flick : pat

9. *battle : defeat* ::
   a. game : loss
   b. contest : opponent
   c. crime : jail
   d. injury : doctor

10. *cloth : clothes* ::
    a. tar : rock
    b. sandwich : bread
    c. boards : buildings
    d. salt : soup

11. *field : game* ::
    a. cook : food
    b. stage : play
    c. sport : athlete
    d. gardener : crop

12. *quiet : calm* ::
    a. sweet : spicy
    b. narrow : wide
    c. boring : dull
    d. sticky : stiff

Analogies

Underline the letter of the pair of words that has the **same relationship** as the numbered pair of words.

1. *concert* : *music* ::
   a. art : show
   b. theatre : play
   c. diner : cook
   d. cards : poker

2. *soda* : *straw* ::
   a. water : boat
   b. plane : clouds
   c. car : garage
   d. bullet : barrel

3. *button* : *zipper* ::
   a. butter : margarine
   b. kitchen : toaster
   c. vitamin : food
   d. needle : cloth

4. *law* : *citizen* ::
   a. weapon : peace
   b. reins : horse
   c. furnace : heat
   d. criminal : judge

5. *study* : *learning* ::
   a. eat : drinking
   b. reading : writing
   c. car : servicing
   d. search : discovering

6. *germ* : *illness* ::
   a. medicines : drug
   b. honey : bee
   c. bomb : explosion
   d. nail : build

7. *mechanic* : *car* ::
   a. bank : teller
   b. swimming : pool
   c. janitor : dump
   d. jeweler : watch

8. *handcuffs* : *robber* ::
   a. leash : dog
   b. rope : laundry
   c. shoes : feet
   d. hydrant : fire

9. *leap* : *tumble* ::
   a. rocket : robot
   b. soar : plunge
   c. kangaroo : frog
   d. jump : fence

10. *fantastic* : *incredible* ::
    a. sincere : eager
    b. stubborn : obedient
    c. simple : plain
    d. confused : clear

11. *manhole* : *well* ::
    a. fence : wall
    b. post : lamp
    c. stairs : building
    d. subway : passenger

12. *follow* : *lead* ::
    a. beg : borrow
    b. catch : throw
    c. hurry : rush
    d. begin : try

Finding Different Meanings

Words often have more than one meaning, and your awareness of these different meanings is an important part of your skill at understanding oral and written language. A good example is the word *run*. How many of its meanings can you think of? Write them on the lines that follow, and then compare your list with the selection of definitions at the bottom of the page* or, even better, with the entries for *run* in your dictionary.

_____

_____

The following exercise explores your ability to think of different meanings of words quickly. It will also help you learn to express meanings accurately.

Directions: Do this exercise in fifteen minutes. Below each word list as many different meanings as you can. Try to find at least three. When you have finished, compare your answers with your classmates' or your teacher's answers.

1. bug: _____

_____

_____

2. club: _____

_____

_____

3. mug: _____

_____

_____

4. game:_____

_____

_____

5. break: _____

_____

*Run: 1) to move at a pace faster than a walk; 2) to flee; 3) to operate; 4) a ravel in a stocking; 5) a score in baseball; 6) a path or course on a ski slope.

Finding Different Meanings

In this exercise one word is used in two different sentences. It has a different meaning in each sentence. Write a definition of the underlined word below each sentence.

Example:

1   He was unable to pay the <u>bill</u>.

  statement of money due

2. The baby bird took the worm from the mother's <u>bill</u>.

  the mouth structure of a bird

Set I:

1. He <u>framed</u> me, but I didn't do it.

2. The <u>frame</u> broke when the picture dropped.

Set II:

1. One <u>boot</u> was missing.

2. They want to <u>boot</u> me out of the club.

Set III:

1. He offered to <u>foot</u> the bill.

2. My robe is on the <u>foot</u> of my bed.

Set IV:

1. He caught the <u>fly</u> deep in right field.

2. Get the <u>fly</u> off the cheese!

Finding Different Meanings

The same word is used in two different sentences. It has a different meaning in each sentence. Write a definition of the underlined word below each sentence.

Set I:

1. The directors will <u>screen</u> the contestants before they choose the ones who will appear on the show.

_____

2. The flies are getting through the holes in the <u>screen</u>.

_____

Set II:

1. Joe gave me a <u>set</u> of darts for Christmas.

_____

2. Marty <u>set</u> the sodas on the table.

_____

Set III:

1. Are the <u>pickles</u> sour or sweet?

_____

2. After the accident last night, Pat was in a <u>pickle</u>.

_____

Set IV:

1. You can remember her phone number if you <u>rack</u> your brain.

_____

2. Mr. Griffin lined up all his clocks on a <u>rack</u>.

_____

Set V:

1. The horse <u>whipped</u> its tail to get flies off its back.

_____

2. The Dodgers <u>whipped</u> the Braves in last night's game.

_____

Words in Context

Since many words have more than one meaning, we must figure out the particular meaning of a word from the way the word is used in the sentence. The exercise below gives you practice figuring out meanings from context.

Each underlined word is *not* used in its most familiar sense. For example, in the first sentence, *face* does not have its most common meaning — the front of the head. What does it mean in that sentence? Write your definition beside the word. You may use a dictionary if you need to.

1. The face of the house could be seen from the road.

   face:_____

2. We watched her eye the newcomer suspiciously.

   eye: _____

3. Susie is a good sport.

   sport: _____

4. If you soil your party dress, you'll have to wash it.

   soil: _____

5. Seymour made a good play at first base.

   play:_____

6. When he took his seat in the crowded stadium, he had to sandwich himself between two men smoking cigars.

   sandwich: _____

7. Don't sink your money into a failing business.

   sink:_____

8. The merchants jack up the prices when the tourists come to town.

   jack up: _____

9. At the start of a race, Bold Beauty has been known to jump the gun.

   jump: _____

10. They went for a spin in the new car.

    spin:_____

Definition

A definition states the meaning of a word. A good definition is clear and exact. Here is an example of a poor definition:

A pencil is something to write with.

The same definition fits a pen or a piece of chalk or a crayon. It is not clear and exact. Here is a better definition:

A pencil is a tool for writing or drawing that has a center made of lead.

Many definitions have two parts. The first part is the class or category of the word. A pencil is not just "something." It is a writing tool.

The second part is a detail that makes the word being defined different from other things in the same class or category. How is a pencil different from other writing tools? It has lead. A pen, for example, uses ink.

Here is a definition of *student* that has the two parts shown above.

A student is a person who attends school.
     (category)   (detail that makes it different from other persons)

Another way to give a good definition is to give a synonym. The synonym should be as close in meaning as possible. It should also be familiar enough so that it helps us understand the original word. If you are told that one meaning of *drag* is *to protract*, do you understand the word *drag* better? Most likely you will not, because *protract* is not a word you are familiar with. Here are examples of synonyms used well to define a word.

To interrogate is to question.
To grapple is to seize and hold.

Here are words for you to define. Use one of the two systems described above.

1. An hour is _____

2. Joyful means _____

3. A tree is _____

4. To glitter is _____

Definition

Some of the definitions given below are good definitions and some are not. Under the good definitions write *good*. Under each poor definition, write a better definition in the space below the sentence.

1. A desk is a table used for reading and writing.

   _____

2. A star is something that shines at night.

   _____

3. To save is to rescue from danger.

   _____

4. A mane is part of a lion.

   _____

5. To float is to be in water.

   _____

6. A brush is an instrument that has bristles and a handle.

   _____

7. A farm is land found in the country.

   _____

8. A kite is flown in the air.

   _____

9. Flat means level or smooth.

   _____

10. Golf is a game played with a small ball.

   _____

Definition

Some of the definitions given below are good definitions and some are not. Write *good* under each good definition. Under each poor definition, write a better definition.

1. A tricycle has three wheels.

   _____

2. A puppet is a small figure of a person or animal moved by hand or by strings.

   _____

3. A flipper is something you wear for swimming quickly.

   _____

4. An octopus is a sea creature with eight arms.

   _____

5. To fling is to throw with force.

   _____

6. A brake is a pedal you step on in a car.

   _____

7. A fingerprint is a mark for identification.

   _____

8. To provide means to equip.

   _____

9. A sponge is used for cleaning up spills.

   _____

10. Hail is lumps of ice.

   _____

Following Directions

This exercise tests your skill in classification as well as in following directions. Use a separate piece of paper. Follow each step carefully.

a. Make three columns on your paper: to do this, draw two vertical lines down the paper about three inches apart.

b. Draw one horizontal line across your paper two inches from the top.

c. Write the following headings in the box at the top of each column: Things that Fly, Things to Write with, and Things with Wheels.

d. In the column under each heading, write down as many things as you can think of that belong in each category.

e. Put your name under the last thing you wrote in the last column, going from right to left.

f. Count the total number of things you put under each of the three headings. If there are more than five things in each column, put a large star under your name. If not, put a question mark beside your name.

Following Directions

Follow this set of directions on the bottom of this page.

a. Write the word "it" in the center of the top part of your answer section.

As you follow the next step and every step after that, write the new word below the old word.

b. Add a letter to "it" that makes a word meaning "take a seat."

c. Add a letter that makes a word meaning "a narrow cut or opening."

d. Add a letter that makes a word meaning "to divide into parts."

e. Add a letter that makes a word meaning "a support for a broken leg or finger." You should now have a six-letter word.

f. Take out two letters to make a word that means "turn around rapidly."

g. Take out a letter to make a word that means "a sharply pointed object used to hold things together."

h. Take out a letter to make a word that is the opposite of "out."

i. Take out a letter to make a word that means "me." Write this word with a capital letter.

Following Directions

Use a separate sheet of paper to follow each set of directions.

Problem 1:

a. Draw a round figure that touches all four edges of your paper.

b. Put a dot in the center of the circle.

c. Make a triangle by connecting the dot to each of the bottom corners of the paper. (The bottom edge will be the third side of the triangle.)

d. Color in the areas of the triangle that are not inside the circle.

e. Write your name inside the circle but outside the triangle.

Problem 2:

a. Put a dot in each corner of your paper.

b. Draw a line between each pair of dots. Make sure you connect every pair.

c. Write the number of lines you just drew in the upper left corner.

d. Put a dot in each corner of your paper.

e. Draw a line from the top left dot to the bottom right dot.

f. Draw a line from the top right dot to the bottom left dot.

g. Write the number of dots you made on your paper in the top right corner.

h. Count the number of separate triangles on your paper that do not overlap each other. Write the number in the bottom left corner.

i. Write your first name on the right side of the bottom of your paper and your last name on the left side of the bottom of your paper.

Following Directions

Use the bottom half of this sheet of paper to follow this set of directions.

a. Print the word *separate* in about the middle of your work area.

b. If *separate* has fewer than eight letters, draw a circle around it.

c. Write the number of vowels in the word over the word. Write the number of different vowels under the word.

d. If the word contains more than six different letters, draw a star in the upper left corner.

e. If the word has inside it a word that means "a kind of rodent larger than a mouse," draw a heart in the lower right corner.

f. If the word has inside it a word meaning "two things that are designed to go together," draw a triangle in the upper right corner.

g. If the word has inside it a word that means "speed," draw a heart in the lower left corner.

h. Try to find other words you can spell with the letters of *separate*.
The letters may be used in any order. Write these words in a column on the right side of your work area. If you can find five or more words, write your name at the top of your work area. If not, write your name at the bottom of the page.

Sentence Meaning

Introduction

This unit of study concentrates on the sentence. A sentence is a unit of language, just as a word is. Although it is made up of a number of words, it can be considered a unit because it expresses one central thought. In order to build this unit, all the words in a sentence are related to each other. For example, *the package* is not yet what we call a complete thought. What about the package, we ask. *The package arrived yesterday.* Now we have a sentence. All of the words are related to each other to express a complete thought.

Here are some things to think about as you start this unit of study:

1. The order of words in a sentence can affect its meaning. Look at how different the meaning is if one or two of the words are in different order.

> The snake bit the horse.
> The horse bit the snake.

> Only children eat cotton candy. (Meaning: Adults don't.)
> Children eat only cotton candy. (Meaning: Children don't eat anything else.)

2. To understand a sentence exactly you must be careful to understand how every word, even small words, contributes to the meaning of the whole. Can you see how the meaning changes in these sentences?

> The postman *always* brings me letters. (not true)
> The postman *sometimes* brings me letters. (true)

Words that may not express the main thought of the sentence may build relationships between parts of the sentence. Can you see how the ideas are related to each other in different ways in these sentences?

> The audience cheered *when* the concert ended.
> The audience cheered *because* the concert ended.

3. Once you get used to the idea of relationships between words and word groups within a sentence, it is helpful to learn to read by phrases. Phrases are word groups that belong together in meaning. There are three phrases in the following sentence:

> The sinking boat was last seen at midnight.
> The sinking boat   was last seen   at midnight.

How many phrases are there in this sentence? _____

> At the bottom of the pond the baby turtle was burrowing into the mud.

Sentence or Not?

Imagine that someone said to you:

Lost her bathing suit.

            or

The man in the dark glasses.

Hearing such incomplete ideas can be both frustrating and confusing. We wonder what the full thought is. *Who* lost her bathing suit? *What about* the man in the dark glasses?

You may remember that a sentence is usually defined as the expression of a complete thought. No essential part is left out. Words in sentences are related to each other in many different ways, but they *are always related* to one another. We can see that something happens to someone or something without being left to wonder what the full thought really is.

The examples above are now sentences:

Al's grandmother lost her bathing suit.

The man in the dark glasses borrowed Sue's skateboard.

In the exercise below label each group of words either **S** for Sentence or **N** for Not a Sentence.

_____ 1. On the top of the shelf by the back door.

_____ 2. Swimming alone at night is dangerous.

_____ 3. When the plumber finally arrived.

_____ 4. Fear of bridges, tunnels, and mountain heights.

_____ 5. Driving through the quiet town at night.

_____ 6. Don't speak out of turn in his class.

_____ 7. The gang took Mickey for a ride.

_____ 8. To explain the answer in more detail.

_____ 9. The cold kept her awake at night.

_____ 10. After Santa Claus leaves your house, call me up.

_____ 11. Running wildly up the alley.

_____ 12. Her beagle ate baked potatoes.

_____ 13. On the last day of the tournament.

_____ 14. Because he was so hungry.

_____ 15. They will paint the garage yellow.

Sentence or Not?

In the exercise below label each group of words **S** if it is a sentence and **N** if it is not a sentence.

_____ 1. Applauded loudly at the end of the concert.

_____ 2. All afternoon he napped on a park bench.

_____ 3. Instead of asking his mother to iron the shirt.

_____ 4. After he heard the advertisement on the radio.

_____ 5. It would start a national crisis.

_____ 6. Looking up, he saw a hawk gliding over the meadow.

_____ 7. The woman who had taken his school picture last year.

_____ 8. Then Betsy saw Ed leaning against the wall.

_____ 9. He gave up taking guitar lessons after that.

_____ 10. All of her teammates, including Beth Palmer.

_____ 11. Every day except Sunday, Ellie swam ten laps in the pool.

_____ 12. Tom wanted his parents to raise his allowance.

_____ 13. Either my brothers or my cousins from New York.

_____ 14. Since he could never remember her phone number.

_____ 15. That night the moon was full and bright.

_____ 16. The last one on the bus.

_____ 17. Larry's cat howled at night.

_____ 18. Miriam helped Wanda tie her shoe.

_____ 19. Sailing on an ice boat.

_____ 20. In the deepest part of the river the trout.

Main Thought

In long sentences the point or main thought is usually expressed in a few key words or phrases. You need to be able to figure out what the main thought is in order to understand the focus and organization of the sentence. See if you can find the main thought in this sentence:

Even though he had lost his camera when he moved to Colorado, Craig signed up for the photography course offered at the high school.

Which of the following would you choose as the main thought?

_____Craig lost his camera.
_____Craig had moved to Colorado.
_____Craig signed up for the photography course.
_____The photography course was offered at the high school.

The main thought is the third choice. The other choices present conditions that help us understand what the situation was when Craig signed up for the course.

The sentences in the exercise below are not as complicated as the example given above. Each sentence has just two parts. One part expresses the main thought; the other doesn't. Underline the part of the sentence that expresses the main thought.

1. When I saw the books he was reading, I could tell he was very smart.

2. The spider waited patiently until a fly got caught in its web.

3. Every dog in the neighborhood stayed away from Magnet because her claws were so sharp.

4. Beth found her mittens long after she had bought a new pair.

5. Hiding on top of the mountain, the spy watched the valley carefully.

6. Our dog and cat are good friends except when the dog gets a bone.

7. Grandmother's nerves haven't settled down since the day the vacuum cleaner exploded.

8. Before I left her house, I made her promise to call me soon.

9. Even though he is your friend, I don't trust him.

10. I borrowed a tuxedo from my Uncle Sam so that I could go to the prom.

11. Looking for a parking space, Marie drove around the block four times.

12. Ralph didn't finish the report even though he worked all weekend.

Main Thought

The purpose of this exercise is to see if you can find the main thought in a sentence. Each sentence has two basic parts. Underline the part of the sentence that expresses the main thought.

1. Mr. Black left town after his wife died.

2. To get to the restaurant we had to drive an hour.

3. Slippery roads mean no school for me because the school bus can't drive up our hill.

4. An hour after the crash the fire was still burning.

5. Keep away from my fort unless you want a punch in the nose.

6. When the drug store put all its candy on sale, every kid in town showed up.

7. Hiding behind the bush, Mike pretended to be a cowboy.

8. All the people in my class pass notes to each other, even though they're not allowed to.

9. Barbara stepped on a garter snake while it was sleeping in a patch of sunlight on the porch.

10. Hanging from a window sill at the top of the building, Batman yelled for help.

11. Under a big pile of garden tools and old boards in the garage, I saw a nest of baby mice.

12. John climbed to the very top of the oak tree in spite of all the warnings Mr. Lester had given him.

13. When Ray slipped on the bridge, his science book fell into the river.

14. The fog rose slowly, hiding the flags and the telephone poles.

15. After eating several handfuls, José put the potato chips into a bowl on the table.

16. The phone rang constantly, although no one was home to answer it.

Getting the Point

The purpose of this exercise is to give you practice finding the main idea of a sentence. Read each sentence. Then read the sentence that follows the word *Point*. If the second sentence gives the main idea of the first sentence, put a check on the line. If it does not restate the point of the sentence, put *No* on the line.

Example:

After breakfast the next morning, two of the boys from the camp went for a swim in the lake even though their counselors had told them not to do so.

Point? Two boys from the camp went for a swim against orders. ___✔___

1. Before the dogs had reached the river, the fox had swum to the other side and disappeared down its hole.

   Point? The dogs reached the river before the fox. _____

2. Mr. Smith disagreed with John's statement that wars are always caused by greed.

   Point? Mr. Smith felt that wars are not always caused by greed. _____

3. Animals of different species are thought of as natural enemies, although many live peacefully side by side.

   Point? Animals of different species are natural enemies. _____

4. As the janitor picked up the dead rat and threw it into the garbage, he thought that some day soon he'd be fired because he was not keeping the building clean enough.

   Point? The janitor thought he'd be fired some day soon. _____

5. On the last day of the circus only the leopard had the energy to put up a struggle when the big cats were put back in their cages.

   Point? The big cats were put back in their cages without a struggle. _____

6. Huddling under dripping trees, Wendy and Leonard used up a package of matches trying to get the campfire lit.

   Point? Wendy and Leonard huddled under the trees to light the campfire. _____

Jumbled Sentences

In the English language the meaning of a sentence is often dependent on the order in which the words appear. Usually, if we change the word order, we also change the meaning of the sentence. For example:

The donkey kicked Aunt Julia.
Aunt Julia kicked the donkey.

We can easily make nonsense out of many sentences by jumbling the word order.

Begin before speaking think they should people.

The exercise below gives you jumbled sentences to unscramble. The purpose is to make you aware of the relationship between word order and meaning in a sentence. Write each sentence so that it makes sense without adding or leaving out any of the words. For example, in correct order the sentence above reads:

People should think before they begin speaking.

1. Never travelled I have anywhere before like this.

   _____

2. The soldiers for home suddenly after the war left.

   _____

3. Cancelled the rain has been our picnic because of.

   _____

4. Trust should a smiling never cat you.

   _____

5. Not foolish on a test is plainly following directions.

   _____

6. Front newspaper newspaper through threw the the the window boy.

   _____

7. Politician the in the every room hand shook.

   _____

Jumbled Sentences

The sentences below contain words out of order. Your job is to change the order of the words so that the sentence makes sense. Do not add or leave out any words. Place the words that you want to emphasize first in the sentence if you can.

1. With taste sauerkraut hotdogs good.

   _____

2. Lost strokes the by he match two golf.

   _____

3. Help flashlight with he his for signaled.

   _____

4. Proudly parade young on marched soliders the.

   _____

5. Not plane could field they on the land the bumpy.

   _____

6. Streamed after through the the rain sunlight clouds.

   _____

7. A both without cross never looking street ways.

   _____

8. Cup don't before first Marie of bother coffee her.

   _____

9. Some eggs put people scrambled their on ketchup.

   _____

10. To fell lake the her of the eyeglasses bottom.

    _____

Phrase Reading

When we read, our eyes do the seeing, and our mind uses the visual information to retrieve the sounds of the words that are represented by the letters. Then it makes sense of the string of words and word groups (called phrases) that the eyes are taking in.

Here is a demonstration that will help you understand how the eyes and the mind work together in reading. First, find a partner for this experiment. Then, use a sharp pencil to make a hole where the circle appears. Next ask your partner to read the paragraph above the circle while you watch the way his or her eyes move looking through the hole from the back of the page. You will see best if you put your eye right up to the hole. Your partner should read at a normal distance from the page.

> The fire alarm sounded at six o'clock in the morning. All of Squad B was ready to roll out the engines by 6:10 when the phone rang and someone informed the firefighters that the fire was already under control. Unfortunately, the caller did not give a name, so the firefighters had no choice but to send out at least one engine to check the situation reported at 10 Union Street.

When you and your partner have seen how each other's eyes move in reading, repeat the process once. This time count the number of times your partner's eyes stop on each line. You should be able to tell when a new line is begun because the eyes make a broad return sweep at that point.

What did you see as your partner read? How many times did his eyes stop and start again as he read each line? If he stopped as many times as there are words, then your friend is reading word by word. If his eyes made fewer stops than the average number of words in each line, then he is reading by phrases.

A phrase is a group of words that are related to each other in meaning. The words in a phrase function as a unit. For example, *her new brown cowboy hat* is a phrase, while *new brown* is not. The mind has an easier time understanding what it reads if reading is done in phrases rather than word by word. In the example below, the words are separated to imitate what it is like for the mind to take in one word at a time and still put together the meaning of the whole sentence. Compare this word-by-word reading with the phrase reading below it.

The	last	leg	of	the	chicken	tasted

salty.

In the last leg	of the race	Lou's horse	pulled ahead.

Phrase Reading

Getting used to natural phrasing will help you improve your understanding of what you read. The purpose of the exercise that follows is to help you learn to recognize phrases as you read. In Exercise 1 there are three phrases in each of the sentences. Draw a line under each phrase. The first one has been done for you. In Exercise 2 there are four phrases in each sentence. Underline each one in the same way.

Exercise 1:

1. Uncle Albert was painting a pink dragon.

2. One battery in the radio was not working.

3. The April snowfall has covered the spring flowers.

4. After the storm the broken wires were repaired.

5. Only Buster will trade old baseball cards.

6. The black dog is snoring under the purple chair.

7. In the fall a deer's rusty coat turns gray.

8. Don't touch the hot pan on the stove.

9. Television comedies cheer up lonely people.

10. May I take a long walk through the woods?

11. My grandfather Emilio traveled alone to America.

12. His favorite present was lost in the wrapping paper.

13. Between matches her new tennis racket was stolen.

Exercise 2:

1. My grandmother Harnell will be sending the old books to the cub scouts.

2. The red sportscar beside the church is owned by my sister.

3. The tall stranger tried to sell my little brother an old bike.

4. An experienced cook can open cherrystone clams with ease.

5. Through the hot summer midday the wise natives slept peacefully in the shade.

Phrase Reading

The story on this page is divided into phrases. Reading it this way will give you practice reading in phrases. Read the story as fast as you can, remembering that you will have a question to answer at the end.

An aviator
      was sent
            on a mission
                  to a distant part
                        of the globe.

When he returned
          to his base,
               he noticed that
                    it was strangely quiet.

Everything was
          in perfect order,
               but there wasn't
                    a sign of life

in the place.
          He wandered
               through town,
                   very surprised.
                        He could not find

even one
      living creature
               in town.
               He tore back
                   to the airport,

filled his plane
          with gas,
             and flew,
               terrified,
                 to New York,
                    London,

and Moscow.
        While he had been
               on his mission,
                   every animal

and human being
    seemed
      to have disappeared
        from the earth.
          He was

the only person
    alive
     in the world!
       He thought
        about the situation
          carefully

and found it
    unbearable.
      Suicide
       seemed to be
        the only solution.

He swallowed
   a few pills
     of deadly poison
       and waited calmly
         for the poison

to take effect.
   Just as the drug
     reached his brain
       and the room
         started swimming

before his eyes,
   he heard
     a familiar sound.
       It was
        the telephone
         ringing.

Question: Why was the ringing of the telephone such a surprise?

Word Order

The order of words affects the meaning of a sentence. To understand the meaning of a sentence fully, the reader must be sensitive to the exact placement of words. Look at the examples below. The words in each sentence are the same, but the placement of *only* changes. As a result, the meaning of the whole sentence is affected.

1. *Only* the baboon ate the banana.
2. The *only* baboon ate the banana.
3. The baboon *only* ate the banana.
4. The baboon ate the *only* banana.
5. The baboon ate the banana *only*.

Only affects the meaning of a word near it. In the first sentence *only* adjusts our understanding of the baboon, but in the last sentence it goes with the word *banana*. Below you have been given the meaning of a few of the word groups that contain *only*. See if you can write down the meaning of the others. Check back to the complete sentences as you need to.

1. *Only the baboon* means: __No other animal ate the banana._____

2. *The only baboon* means: _____

3. The baboon *only ate* the banana means: ___He didn't do anything else to the banana__

(he didn't throw it or squish it). _____

4. *The only banana* means: _____

5. *The banana only* means: _____

Now read the two pairs of sentences below. Explain the difference in the meaning in each pair.

Set I:
    a) Only the window was open a crack.
    b) The window was open only a crack.

_____

_____

Set II:
    a) Just the secretary left the office at five o'clock.
    b) The secretary left the office at just five o'clock.

_____

_____

Word Order

Read the first sentence. Think about its meaning, paying particular attention to such small words as *only*. Then read the three choices given below, looking for the one that most closely shows the meaning of the original sentence. Put the letter of this sentence on the line.

_____ 1. Barbara only washed the strawberries.

  a. No one else washed the strawberries.
  b. Barbara did not do anything to the strawberries but wash them.
  c. Barbara didn't wash the rest of the fruit.

_____ 2. Sam left just his dog at the kennel.

  a. Sam left his dog but not his other pets at the kennel.
  b. Sam didn't leave his dog anywhere except the kennel.
  c. Sam was the only person who left his dog at the kennel.

_____ 3. Aunt Millie grew even mushrooms in her closet.

  a. Lots of people grew mushrooms in their closets.
  b. Aunt Millie grew many different plants in her closet.
  c. Aunt Millie grew plants all over her house.

_____ 4. After almost five hours the chimney sweep had finished the job.

  a. The chimney sweep finished the job in a little less than five hours.
  b. The chimney sweep hadn't quite finished the job.
  c. The chimney sweep took more than five hours to complete the job.

_____ 5. The post office sold only twenty-cent stamps in the afternoon.

  a. You could buy ten-cent stamps in the afternoon.
  b. You could buy twenty-cent stamps just in the afternoon.
  c. The one stamp sold in the afternoon was a twenty-cent stamp.

_____ 6. George just ate the pickled herring.

  a. No one else ate the pickled herring.
  b. George would only eat pickled herring.
  c. Right at this time George has finished eating the pickled herring.

Word Order

One word is moved in each set of sentences in this exercise. Below each set there are three possible meanings. Match each sentence with the statement that expresses the same meaning by placing the number of the sentence next to it. The first one has been started for you.

Set I:
1. Only Sam helped the coach clean up the locker room after practice on Fridays.
2. Sam helped the coach clean up the locker room after practice only on Fridays.

___1___ None of the other players helped the coach clean the locker room.

_____ Sam didn't help the coach clean up other areas of the gym.

_____ Sam didn't clean the locker room with the coach on Tuesdays.

Set II:
1. Even if it rains on Saturday, we'll go to the aquarium.
2. If it rains on Saturday, we'll even go to the aquarium.

_____ We won't go to the aquarium if it rains on Saturday.

_____ We'll go to lots of places including the aquarium if it rains Saturday.

_____ We'll got to the aquarium whether or not it rains on Saturday.

Set III:
1. Aviators like pizza with just anchovies.
2. Just aviators like pizza with anchovies.

_____ Aviators like eating pizza with nothing but anchovies on top.

_____ Aviators like pizza that doesn't have too many anchovies on top.

_____ No one except aviators likes to eat pizza with anchovies.

Set IV:
1. Some of the kids went with Angela to the science fiction movies.
2. The kids went to some of the science fiction movies with Angela.

_____ The kids didn't go to all of the movies.

_____ Angela went to all of the science fiction movies.

_____ Not all the kids went to the movies with Angela.

Word Order

Change the order of the words in each sentence so that the sentence has the meaning given in the parentheses. *Do not add or leave out any words.*

1. Only Sam knew the answer to the problem. (Reorder the words in the sentence so that we know there aren't several possible answers to the problem.)

   _____

   _____

2. Only Sam knows the answer to the problem. (Reorder the words so that we know there is just one problem.)

   _____

   _____

3. My grandmother just went to the early movie. (Reorder the words in the sentence so that the grandmother is the only person who went to the movie.)

   _____

   _____

4. My grandmother just went to the early movie. (Reorder the words in the sentence so that we know grandmother didn't go anywhere except to the early movie.)

   _____

   _____

5. Only Liz gave the twins help learning to ride their bikes. (Reorder the words so that we learn that Liz didn't help anyone but the twins.)

   _____

   _____

6. Tim was too happy to think about the cost of the dinner party. (Reorder the words so that we learn that Tim was another person who cared about the cost of the dinner party.)

   _____

   _____

Word Order

Change the order of the words in each sentence so that the sentence reflects the idea given in the parentheses. *Do not add or leave out any words.*

1. I heard only John shouting at the boys.
    a. (Reorder the words so that we know no one else heard John shouting.)

    _____

    _____

    b. (Reorder the words so that it suggests John wasn't shouting at the girls, too.)

    _____

    _____

2. He decorated the room simply. (Reorder the words so that we know the only thing he did to the room was decorate it.)

    _____

    _____

3. People handle few poisonous snakes. (Reorder the words so that we know some but not many people handle poisonous snakes.)

    _____

    _____

4. Some students on the cheerleading squad refused to wear their outfits to practices. (Reorder the words so that we know the students would not wear their outfits to all of the practices.)

    _____

    _____

5. The mailcarrier just delivered a letter to Tess. (Reorder the words so that we know the mailcarrier gave Tess a letter, but nothing else.)

    _____

    _____

Small Words

As we read, some words are bound to seem more important to us than others. We seem to focus naturally on names and actions. Sometimes, though, we don't pay close enough attention to the small words, and so we may misunderstand the meaning of the sentence. Examples of important small words are.

when   at   since   after   in   beyond

Words like that play an important role because they show relationships of time (*after, when*), space (*under, beyond*), or condition (*because, since, if*).

The following exercise will give you experience working out the meaning of sentences that contain small words. Working on these sentences should make you aware of the importance of understanding small words exactly as they work in each sentence.

Read the two sentences you are given for each problem. Then read the question that follows. Pick the sentence that answers the question correctly. Put the number of the sentence in the blank. The first one is done for you.

A. 1. The toothpaste is on the third shelf beside the soap.
   2. The toothpaste is under the soap on the third shelf.

Which sentence suggests you'll have to move the soap to get out a tube of toothpaste? __2__

B. 1. Susan will get her driver's license if she learns to parallel park.
   2. Susan will get her driver's license before she learns to parallel park.

Which sentence suggests that Susan had better learn to parallel park so that she can get her driver's license? _____

C. 1. Sue Smith plays golf whenever she travels.
   2. Sue Smith plays golf except when she travels.

Which sentence tells you that Sue Smith plays golf when she is at home? _____

D. 1. Since you have helped me, I'll talk to John for you.
   2. After you have helped me, I'll talk to John for you.

Which sentence suggests that you have already helped the speaker? _____

E. 1. Do not fill in column 2 if you have filled in column 1.
   2. Do not fill in column 2 until you have filled in column 1.

Which sentence directs you to fill in both columns, column 1 and then column 2? _____

F. 1. Five seconds after the bell rings, press the release button.
   2. Press the release button for five seconds after the bell rings.

In which sentence is there a five-second gap between the bell and the pushing of the release button? _____

G. 1. The drug store is on the street beyond the bank and the post office.
2. The drug store is on the street between the bank and the post office.
Which sentence tells you that the bank and the post office aren't side by side on the same block? _____

H. 1. Paul was upset when he realized that his locker was not near Otto's.
2. Paul was upset when he realized that his locker was not next to Otto's.
Which sentence tells us that Paul's and Otto's lockers were some distance apart? _____

I. 1. Ellen will continue interrupting people unless you stop her.
2. Ellen will continue interrupting people though you stop her.
Which sentence suggests that stopping Ellen will not make her change the way she acts? _____

J. 1. Charlie Brown told us we'd better speak to Lucy while she was in a bad mood.
2. Charlie Brown told us we'd better speak to Lucy before she gets in a bad mood.
In which sentence does Charlie Brown warn us to stay away from Lucy when she is crabby? _____

K. 1. If you make a pie from those green apples, add extra sugar.
2. Since you are making a pie from those green apples, add extra sugar.
In which sentence are we certain that the person is making a pie from the green apples? _____

L. 1. She was unable to help us unless we could pay for the repairs.
2. She was unable to help us if we could pay for the repairs.
In which sentence do we need to have money enough for the repairs in order to get help? _____

M. 1. Neither of the girls can fit into Joe's pairs of cowboy boots.
2. The girls can fit into neither of Joe's pairs of cowboy boots.
Which sentence suggests there are two girls trying on Joe's cowboy boots? _____

Small Words

This exercise is based on small words that have to do with *amount*, such as:

few   **many**   **most**   **fewer than**   **as many as**

Read the situation presented below. Then using the information you are given, label each of the statements **true, false,** or **can't tell.**

Burke's Bowling Alley was running such a thriving business last year that the owner, Mrs. Burke, decided to double the number of lanes in the alley. She added six lanes. Two were for tenpins, and the remainder were for duckpins.

_____ 1. The bowling alley had no more than six lanes at the beginning.

_____ 2. Mrs. Burke added fewer than four lanes for duckpins.

_____ 3. Most of the total number of lanes in the bowling alley are for duckpins.

_____ 4. There are twice as many lanes this year as there were last year.

_____ 5. There are no fewer than two lanes for tenpins in the whole alley.

_____ 6. Many more people are bowling at Burke's this year.

_____ 7. More of the new lanes are for tenpins than for duckpins.

_____ 8. Some crazy guy tried bouncing bowling balls on one of the new lanes for tenpins. It was damaged so badly that it couldn't be used. After that there were not as many new lanes as old ones working.

_____ 9. After that there were more new lanes in working order for tenpins than for duckpins.

_____ 10. As many as five lanes for tenpins were still in use, counting old and new lanes.

Relationships — Cause

Over the next few pages we are going to be looking at different ways that ideas are usually related to each other in sentences. The first of these is **cause-effect**. The term cause-effect means that one thing makes another happen.

> The ice cream was left on the kitchen counter, so it melted.

What *caused* the ice cream to melt? _____

What was the *effect* of leaving the ice cream sitting on the counter? It melted.

The sentences below will give you practice finding the cause of an event. In each sentence, underline the cause.

1. Since Nathan lost his wallet, he couldn't go to the movies.

2. The airplane was circling above the airport because the fog was so thick.

3. Saul had eaten so much Halloween candy that he felt sick.

4. With the thick curtains drawn the room was very dark.

Events that follow each other in time are not necessarily related by cause-effect. We must be careful not to assume that two events are related by causation. Here is an example.

> After the basketball game Margot had a headache.

We cannot say that the basketball game caused Margot's headache. All we know is that the two events occured one after the other.

Exercise: Sort out the sentences that contain a cause-effect relationship from those that don't. Label each sentence that has a cause-effect relationship **CE**.

_____ 1. By the time Glen climbed on board the ferry, it was about to leave the dock.

_____ 2. Before the boat left the harbor, the trip was calm.

_____ 3. The wind and waves on the open sea made the boat pitch and roll.

_____ 4. Because of the movement of the boat, Glen felt sick.

_____ 5. Glen drank a soda so that his stomach felt less queasy.

_____ 6. Once he landed on the island, Glen was happy to sit on the hotel porch and just watch the wild sea.

Relationships — Time Order

When the ideas in a sentence emphasize the order or sequence of events, we call the relationship **time order**. Focusing on a single event, we can talk about what happened before, after, or at the same time as that event. Here is an event: Kelly won the photography contest. Here are sentences built around this event to illustrate time order relationships.

Kelly was sure she had not entered her best photographs before she won the photography contest.

While the judges were looking at the photographs, Kelly went for a walk with her brother.

After she won the photography contest, Kelly applied for a job on the city newspaper.

Exercise: Two things happen in each of the following sentences. Underline the part of the sentence that tells what happens *first*.

1. The two kings quarreled bitterly for years before the war started.

2. The two kings quarreled bitterly for years after the war ended.

3. Before he climbed into the boat, John fastened the rope securely.

4. After it had rained for an hour, it started to snow.

5. The fire had been out of control for an hour before anyone thought to call the fire department.

6. For an hour Karen waited at the corner for the bus, and then she decided to walk to school.

7. Before the flood waters rose, the Steins moved out of the house.

8. Joan took up riding gliders after she had passed the parachuting test.

9. Matthew is playing in a tennis match at 3 o'clock, but before that he has to take his neighbor's children to the dentist.

Relationships

The ideas in each of the sentences below are related either by cause-effect or by time order. Read the sentence carefuly. Then label it either **CE** for cause-effect or **TO** for time order.

_____ 1. The forest fire started because someone left a campfire smoldering.

_____ 2. Before he left for New York, Mr. Dow picked up his suit from the cleaners.

_____ 3. Since she forgot to take her umbrella, Helen ended up sopping wet.

_____ 4. George had picked out a present for Mary a month before her birthday.

_____ 5. The druggist told Mrs. Swanson all the local gossip while he rang up the prices on the cash register.

_____ 6. I knew the dog wouldn't bite me because he was wagging his tail.

_____ 7. As Jeff was crossing the street, an ambulance raced around the corner.

_____ 8. Since their well ran dry, they had to buy bottled water.

_____ 9. The stairs were so steep that everyone had trouble climbing them.

_____ 10. Before the new tenants arrived, the carpenters repaired the broken door.

_____ 11. Mrs. LeMoins designed houses with solar heating for years until she bought the Natural Foods Shop.

_____ 12. The cat jumped on the counter so easily that Mr. Vallery could never leave food sitting there.

_____ 13. When the phone rang, Sharon was in the shower.

_____ 14. Unfortunately, grandmother is too lame to dance.

_____ 15. The two friends met at the Douglas farm and then hiked in the mountains in New Hampshire.

Relationships — Comparison

As you have seen, two ways that ideas can be related to each other in a sentence are cause-effect and time order. A third type of relationship is **comparison.** When one thing is compared to another, likenesses and differences are pointed out. In this example a difference is stated. What is this difference?

Otters swim faster than beavers.

In the next sentence a similarity (likeness) between two things is shown. What is the similarity?

Both animals and reptiles are apt to hiss when threatened.

Exercise: In each of the following sentences, underline the two things that are being compared. Then write **S** on the line if the comparison shows a similarity, or **D** on the line if the comparison shows a difference.

1. Beth has more rings than Mary has. _____

2. I like pens with blue ink, but Doug likes pens with green ink. _____

3. Both football and hockey players wear pads to protect their bodies. _____

4. Jazz is pleasanter than rock to listen to for a long time. _____

5. Margarine is just as fattening as butter. _____

6. Father says the TV uses more electricity than the radio. _____

7. Andy and Mike have red down vests that are almost identical. _____

8. Renee would rather read a mystery than a romance. _____

9. Roses are red, but violets are blue. _____

10. The fire department has a special emergency telephone number; so does the police department. _____

11. Long-haired dogs are more comfortable in northern climates than in southern climates. _____

12. Pike and pickerel are both freshwater fish. _____

13. Most of us saved our energy for the practice, but the twins jogged from the school to the soccer field every day. _____

Relationships

Read each sentence. Figure out how the ideas in the sentence are related to each other. Label the sentence with one of the following relationships: **CE** for cause-effect, **C** for comparison, or **TO** for time order.

_____ 1. Since Michael spent his allowance on baseball cards, he couldn't go to the movies with his friends.

_____ 2. Climbing stairs is more exercise than riding an escalator.

_____ 3. After the trails have been cleared, we'll take the children horseback riding in the mountains.

_____ 4. Ben refused to join Sally at the lunch table because he found George's table manners so awful.

_____ 5. The two brothers were both good-natured, but they fought like enemies when they played tennis.

_____ 6. I didn't get a chance to mow the lawn yesterday because it rained all day.

_____ 7. After the snowstorm let up, Jadine went to see her grandmother in the hospital.

_____ 8. Mr. Swanson says that the reason Mr. Tull's business failed was that his store was not on a busy street.

_____ 9. For centuries people believed that the earth was the center of the universe, but finally astronomers discovered that the earth and other planets circle the sun.

_____ 10. While it is true that most spiders spin webs to trap their food, some, such as the tarantula, capture their victims with deadly bites instead.

Relationships — Examples

Can you give three examples of nighttime occupations?

Notice that examples are concrete or specific members of a general group, in this case jobs people do at night. Sometimes examples are specific instances of a general idea. The important value of examples is that they *are* specific, and they give clear, concrete reference points. In the following sentence, circle the general category and underline the examples.

> Three members of the Kelly family hold nighttime jobs — one as a night watchman, one as a nurse, and one as a telephone operator.

Some of the words or phrases commonly used to introduce examples are:

for example   such as   including   like

Exercise: The following sentences give examples. Read each sentence. Then circle the general category and underline the examples.

1. Brett wears only simple clothes such as blue jeans and work shirts.

2. Jane took her favorite games on the trip, including word puzzles and cards.

3. Last night Mary's smart little sister showed us groups of stars that had special names like Orion, the Big Dipper, and the Milky Way.

4. When I asked her about places she likes to go for vacation, she listed New York, Florida, and Cape Cod.

5. Father gives me too many long jobs to do on Sundays — for example, mowing the whole lawn and washing and waxing the car.

6. Ken and Betsy took their smallest pets to the kindergarten pet fair — Mike the Gypsy Moth, Sperry the Spider, and Grace the Garter Snake, among others.

7. Potato chips, crackers, and popcorn still seem to be people's favorite snacks.

Relationships

Read each sentence. Figure out how the ideas in the sentence are related to each other. Label the sentence with one of the following relationships: **CE** for cause-effect, **TO** for time order, **C** for comparison, or **EX** for examples.

_____ 1. Since she had missed her plane connection, she had to spend the night in a hotel in Detroit.

_____ 2. The postmaster sorted the mail much faster than I ever could have.

_____ 3. After we paddled across the lake, we had to carry the canoe for two exhausting miles.

_____ 4. Coffee doesn't have as much caffeine as tea, I hear.

_____ 5. Mildred has a collection of strange pets, including white rats, parrots, and a python.

_____ 6. Bored and tired, he sat in the car while his mother shopped for two hours.

_____ 7. I refused to climb to the top of the tower because I am afraid of heights.

_____ 8. My parents keep telling me that candy is bad for me, but I think it tastes good and gives me quick energy.

_____ 9. Watching television and reading old magazines are two of the ways I really waste time.

_____ 10. She had picked all the tomatoes off her plants before the first frost came.

_____ 11. They talked about visiting islands on their honeymoon, such as the Virgin Islands or the Caribbean Islands.

_____ 12. Nicole was so spoiled that she never cleared her own dirty dishes.

_____ 13. Hampton polished his uncle's new car until he could see his own reflection on it.

_____ 14. The coach wanted Anne to play in the game, but the trainer argued that her ankle was badly sprained.

_____ 15. The second eruption of the volcano was as violent as the first.

Relationships

All of the sentences below are about sharks. Read each sentence and think how the ideas in the sentence are related. The relationships in the sentences are cause-effect, comparison, or examples. In two of the sentences, there are two relationships within the sentence. Label the relationship, using the following abbreviations: **CE** for cause-effect, **C** for comparison, and **EX** for examples. Remember to give *two* answers for sentences 5 and 6.

_____ 1. Many sharks rip and tear their prey because they have a large number of very sharp teeth.

_____ 2. Sharks have skeletons made of rubbery material called cartilage, in contrast to other fishes whose skeletons are made of hard bone.

_____ 3. Sharks can be a number of different colors, including dark blue, black, yellow-brown, and white.

_____ 4. The smallest sharks (dogfish) are about one foot long, while the great whale shark sometimes reaches a length of fifty feet.

_____
_____ 5. While many of the larger sharks are dangerous to people, others, such as the whale shark and the dogfish, are quite harmless.

_____
_____ 6. Several kinds of sharks are feared because they occasionally attack swimmers without cause; these include the white shark, the tiger shark, and the hammerhead.

_____ 7. Tiger sharks have been known to eat just about anything in the water, including garbage, metal objects, and people.

_____ 8. A lot of people fear sharks because they saw the gory scenes of sharks killing people in *Jaws*.

Key Words and Generalizations

A generalization is a general statement that is based on particular facts. Such a statement is made about a whole group or about a part of a group. Here is an example:

All cats have long tails.

The group in this generalization is cats, and the statement tells us that *every* cat has a long tail. Since we know that bobcats are members of the cat family and don't have long tails, we can tell that this generalization is not a good one.

Now look at two other generalizations about cats:

No cats have long tails.
Some cats have long tails.

In the same way that we examined the first generalization, we can come to the conclusion that the second generalization is not a good one, but the third one is. Can you explain why?

The only words that change in these generalizations are *all, some,* and *no*. These are called **key words**. They are an important part of generalizations because they tell us how much of the group is supposed to fit the particular statement. Key words can also tell us how often the statement is supposed to occur. Here is an example:

Snakes *never* have legs.

All, no, some, and *never* are commonly used key words. Others are:

many   most   every   often   always   sometimes   usually

Sometimes *all* is implied in generalizations, not stated. For example, the generalization "Human beings need food to live." means "*All* human beings need food to live."

Anyone who wants to learn to think clearly should pay attention to the way people use and misuse generalizations. The examples below show how people use generalizations when they speak. Are you willing to accept these generalizations as true? Or are some of them false? Circle the key words in each one, and be ready to discuss why you have labeled each one true or false.

_____ 1. All nurses are kind people.

_____ 2. No girls can play hockey well.

_____ 3. Eating fresh vegetables always makes a person feel healthy.

_____ 4. Politicians are always ambitious.

_____ 5. Good taxi drivers are never held up at stop lights.

Generalizations

Below you will find a series of generalizations. Circle the **key word** in each generalization. Then label the statement **true** or **false**.

_____ 1. All houses have chimneys.

_____ 2. Two plus two never makes five.

_____ 3. A week sometimes has fewer than seven days in it.

_____ 4. Most Canadians live in Canada.

_____ 5. Some wild animals do not die of old age.

_____ 6. Friends often help each other.

_____ 7. A baseball player sometimes wears a mitt.

_____ 8. Every newspaper is printed daily.

_____ 9. No coins are bigger than a quarter.

_____ 10. Clouds always bring rain.

_____ 11. Many summer flowers are yellow.

Think of a key word to put in each of the statements given below to make the generalization **true**. Write the sentence with the key word you have chosen on the line.

1. Bottles are made of glass. _____

2. Triangles have three sides. _____

3. Worms can fly. _____

4. Snow falls in summer. _____

5. Fire gives off heat. _____

Generalizations

There are some generalizations that we cannot fairly label either true or false. Some of these reflect ideas that we truly could not test to determine their truth.

>Most people change their minds about something ten times a day.

Most means more than half. There is no reasonable way to figure out how many times more than half the people change their minds.

Another type of generalization we can't call true or false involves personal taste.

>Most women like little babies.

And a third type is one that uses words that different people would interpret in different ways.

>People usually like cute babies.

What makes a baby cute? Different people will have quite different ideas about a word like "cute."

Exercise: There are ten generalizations below. Five of them should be labeled **CT** for "can't tell." Label the other statements **T** for "true" or **F** for "false."

_____ 1. Most women like men with beards.

_____ 2. All carpets are made of wool.

_____ 3. Cats usually wear collars.

_____ 4. A quarter and two pennies always make 27 cents.

_____ 5. Students usually like math more than science.

_____ 6. Short hair is usually prettier than long hair.

_____ 7. Tomorrow will have twenty-four hours in it.

_____ 8. Some clocks today do not have hands.

_____ 9. All baseball players prefer doughnuts to bagels.

_____ 10. Every living fish is found in water.

_____ 11. Orange juice is always more popular than grapefruit juice.

_____ 12. Usually mystery stories have exciting endings.

Generalizations

Read each generalization. Circle the key word. Write **T** next to each statement that is true and **F** next to each statement that is false. Label the statements you can't call either true or false **CT**.

_____ 1. Not all people born in France speak French.

_____ 2. Circles are always round.

_____ 3. Girls never like to play checkers.

_____ 4. Most teachers like to coach sports.

_____ 5. All trees are living plants.

_____ 6. Many dogs can swim.

_____ 7. Soldiers never fight in peacetime.

_____ 8. No month in the year has more than thirty-one days.

_____ 9. All pet collars are found on dogs.

_____ 10. Homemade cookies usually taste better than store-bought cookies.

_____ 11. Bears do not always walk on two feet.

_____ 12. All snakes are poisonous.

_____ 13. Some tables do not have four legs.

_____ 14. Wet grass is always a sign of recent rain.

_____ 15. Bricks support more weight than concrete.

_____ 16. Every cat has kittens.

_____ 17. Not all seagulls are found at sea.

_____ 18. Tears always mean sadness.

_____ 19. Eagles usually hate hawks.

_____ 20. Some flowers bloom in winter.

Generalizations

Read each generalization. Label the false statements **F** and the can't tell statements **CT**. Leave the true statements blank.

_____ 1. All criminals have broken at least one law.

_____ 2. Lazy people never lead successful lives.

_____ 3. No human being can survive a heart attack.

_____ 4. Tigers are usually more dangerous than rattlesnakes.

_____ 5. Strong winds sometimes damage crops.

_____ 6. Not all Indians come from India.

_____ 7. Blushing is always caused by embarrassment.

_____ 8. Every person must be able to see in order to read.

_____ 9. Glasses are usually worn to improve one's appearance.

_____ 10. The word _bug_ does not always mean insect.

_____ 11. Every father is a human being.

_____ 12. Some brushes aren't used for grooming one's hair.

_____ 13. Every well is dug to find water.

_____ 14. Most young children like fried eggs.

_____ 15. An island is always a body of water completely surrounded by land.

_____ 16. Four books wrapped together for mailing frequently make a six-sided package.

_____ 17. Uncles are never younger than their nephews.

_____ 18. Not every head is on a body.

_____ 19. It is not true that the earth is flat.

_____ 20. Some astronauts wish they were young boys.

Generalizations

Read each generalization. Label the true statements **T** and the false statements **F**. Put an **O** next to the can't tell statements.

_____ 1. People usually complain about uncomfortable chairs.

_____ 2. All spiders have more than three legs.

_____ 3. Few people eat turnips.

_____ 4. Most bread is made from wheat.

_____ 5. All athletes know how to play ice hockey.

_____ 6. Shadows usually disappear at nightfall.

_____ 7. Most overweight people like lemonade.

_____ 8. All soups are served hot.

_____ 9. Some trucks have more than four wheels.

_____ 10. The earth will always support living things.

_____ 11. Sometimes snow falls when the sky is cloudy.

_____ 12. Every planet in our solar system is the same size.

_____ 13. Machines never work properly when you most need them.

_____ 14. Ducks will often perch on telephone wires to rest.

_____ 15. People sometimes do things they later regret.

_____ 16. Plants are the only living things that require water to survive.

_____ 17. Most people with red hair eat carrots.

_____ 18. Summer weather is always warm and sunny.

_____ 19. Every person can have only one birth date.

_____ 20. Comic books are enjoyable reading for most people.

Same or Different Meaning

Read the two sentences in each problem. If the sentences mean the same thing, write **S** on the line. If they have different meanings, leave the line blank.

_____ 1. A. Put the board in place while the glue is hardening.
          B. Before the glue has hardened, put the board in place.

_____ 2. A. Kim wanted to earn $100 in order to buy a bike.
          B. Kim wanted to earn $100 before she bought a bike.

_____ 3. A. One of the few houses that escaped damage in the hurricane was the Joneses'.
          B. Not many houses escaped damage in the hurricane, but the Joneses' was one that did.

_____ 4. A. Although the wind was strong, they went sailing.
          B. They went sailing since the wind was strong.

_____ 5. A. When I asked her who had applied for the job today, she said, ''Just another guy.''
          B. She told me that ''just another guy'' had applied for the job today.

_____ 6. A. You may think that weeding a garden is fun, but it's really hard work.
          B. You're wrong if you think weeding a garden is anything but hard work.

_____ 7. A. Only Mr. Smith believed that most of the hockey players were good skaters.
          B. It was Mr. Smith's belief that the hockey team had many good skaters.

_____ 8. A. The length of the child's foot showed she would be a tall adult.
          B. The child's foot was as long as an adult's.

_____ 9. A. Uncle Seth took Carrie's skateboard away after she broke her wrist.
          B. Carrie broke her wrist, so Uncle Seth took her skateboard away.

_____ 10. A. Keith Blaine plants as many as a dozen kinds of vegetables in his garden.
          B. In his garden, Keith Blaine has up to a dozen plants, all vegetables.

_____ 11. A. Most of Tim's chocolate chip cookies were eaten during the movie.
          B. A few of Tim's chocolate chip cookies were left after the movie.

Same or Different Meaning

Below are some pairs of sentences. Your job is to figure out whether the two sentences in each pair mean the same thing. If they do, mark the pairs **S** (for same). If they do not, mark the pair **NS** (for not the same).

_____ 1. A. A country at war is seldom calm.
        B. Seldom is a country at war calm.

_____ 2. A. No nation is without boundaries.
        B. Every nation has boundaries.

_____ 3. A. A truck often has more than four wheels.
        B. Often a truck has as many as four wheels.

_____ 4. A. Since you've raked the lawn, I'll help you clean the garage.
        B. I'll help you clean the garage when you've raked the lawn.

_____ 5. A. The woman took the only seat in the last row.
        B. Only the woman took a seat in the last row.

_____ 6. A. I asked the painters to paint my white house.
        B. I asked the painters to paint my house white.

_____ 7. A. Most people prefer sailboats to motorboats.
        B. People usually prefer sailboats to motorboats.

_____ 8. A. Do not turn the dial higher than 4 unless the temperature gauge in the refrigerator reads warmer than 40 degrees.
        B. If the temperature gauge in the refrigerator reads 41 degrees or more, turn the dial up past 4.

_____ 9. A. Matthew refuses to drive when the fog is thick.
        B. Until the fog is thick, Matthew refuses to drive.

_____ 10. A. Jane's brother gave the picture of the seashell a title.
        B. Jane's brother gave a title to the picture of the seashell.

_____ 11. A. Melinda painted the living room yellow for her father.
        B. For her father Melinda painted the yellow living room.

_____ 12. A. Since he was not able to take the typing course, he signed up to be in the school play.
        B. He was not able to take the typing course because he signed up to be in the school play.

_____ 13. A. Most people thought that Tim had published many of his stories, but in fact he had sold only one.

B. Tim had sold only one of his stories for publication though most people did not know this.

_____ 14. A. Often Mrs. Fisher ate only a salad for dinner.

B. Mrs. Fisher frequently ate nothing but a salad for dinner.

_____ 15. A. Until my car is repaired, I won't be able to come to see you.

B. I can't come to see you unless my car is fixed.

_____ 16. A. If there are fewer than five people at the meeting, pass out only the first of the reports.

B. If there are only four people at the meeting, pass out the reports first.

_____ 17. A. Juan shaved his beard as well as his mustache to please his girlfriend.

B. Because he wanted to please his girlfriend, Juan shaved both his beard and his mustache.

Following Directions

Use a separate piece of paper to follow this set of directions. Your piece of paper should be about the same size and shape as this piece.

a. Draw a line from the center of the top of the page to the center of the right hand edge.

b. Draw a line from your starting point to the center of the left hand edge.

c. Draw a line from the end of this line to the center of the bottom.

d. Connect this point with the line that ends on the right edge.

e. If the figure you have drawn is not a square, draw a line across the center of your paper. If it is a square, put an X on the second line you drew.

f. If there are more than four triangles on your page, draw a line from the top center to the bottom center. (Edges of the paper can count as sides of triangles.) If there are fewer than four triangles, put a star in the upper right corner.

g. If your paper now has four rectangles on it (again, using edges of the page as sides), write yes in the lower left corner.

h. Write your name along the first line you drew.

Following Directions

Follow this set of directions on the bottom half of this page. Pretend that today is Wednesday, November 10th.

a. Print your name at the bottom of the page in the middle.

b. Today is Wednesday. If tomorrow is not Tuesday, draw a large square in the center of your paper. If it is Tuesday, draw a large circle in the same place.

c. If the day after tomorrow is Friday, draw a diamond inside the figure you have just made. If not, make a star inside the figure you have just made.

d. Draw an arrow through your design if yesterday was Tuesday, the 9th of November. If it wasn't, draw an arrow through your last name.

e. If the day before yesterday was not Monday, draw a heart in the lower left corner of the page. Draw a heart around the design you have made so far if it was.

Following Directions

Using the bottom half of this page, follow this set of directions.

a. Draw a line from the lower left corner to the upper right corner of your paper.
b. Put a dot in the middle of the line.
c. Draw a line from this dot to the lower right corner.
d. Put a dot in the middle of this line.
e. Draw a line from the second dot to the upper right corner of your paper.
f. Draw a line from the first dot to a corner that has no lines.
g. Put a dot in the center of the last line you drew. Draw a line between this dot and the lower left corner.
h. Print your name along the first line you drew.

Following Directions

Follow this set of directions on the bottom section of this page.

a. Print your first name in large letters in the center of the section.

b. Suppose Chris is Amy's older brother and Beth is Amy's sister. If Amy is older than Chris, circle the first letter of your name. If Amy is younger than Chris, circle the last letter of your name.

c. If Beth is Chris's brother, underline your name. If she is not, put a star under the circle you drew.

d. If Beth is younger than Amy, put a heart above the second letter of your name. If she is older than Amy, put a star under the first letter of your name. If you can't tell whether she is older or younger than Amy, put a circle before your name.

e. Beth is taller than Amy but she is shorter than Chris. Put a box around everything you have drawn so far if Chris is not the tallest of the three. Put a circle around everything if he is the tallest.

f. If Amy is not the shortest, put a heart over the second letter of your name. If she is the shortest, put a triangle under the first letter of your name.

Following Directions

Use the bottom of this paper to follow this set of directions. When you are asked to count letters, always count from left to right.

a. Print your name at the center of the bottom of the page.

b. Near the top of your paper print IAMGOODAT. With each step in the directions, print all the letters, old and new, under the last set of letters you wrote after you have made the changes indicated.

c. Put the letters of the word WIN after the third letter.

d. Take out the first A. Put two Ls where the A was. Take out the second A. Put RC where the A was.

e. Move the two Os. Put one before and one after the two Ls. Then put a third O at the end of the sequence of letters.

f. Move the first I. Put it after the D. Add another I, putting it after the T.

g. Add an E after the twelfth letter. Take out the M.

h. Put an F at the beginning and NS at the end of the letter sequence.

Paragraph Structure and Meaning

Introduction

The language units we have studied so far are the word and the sentence. Words go together to make sentences; sentences go together to make paragraphs. We notice paragraphs because of their shape. A new paragraph is indented or set off with extra space between paragraphs, as in this workbook.

It is the content of the paragraph that really makes it a unit. With this in mind, some questions may occur to you. How do you know when to start a new paragraph? How do you know which sentences should go in one paragraph and which ones should be put in a different paragraph?

Here are several important points that should help you to begin to understand the nature of a paragraph.

1. A paragraph is about one main idea. When a different main idea is presented, a new paragraph begins.

    Can you tell where a new paragraph should start in the following set of sentences?

    The man opened the door slowly and silently. He peered in carefully and then slid into the room sideways. His hat was pulled down over his forehead and his right hand was in his coat pocket. John and I decided the man was a spy. Since John and I had to get to class, we kept walking down the hall. When we reached the secretary's office, we told her we had seen a really strange man sneaking into the science lab. She laughed. The man was her husband, and he was also the district's fire inspector!

2. Only sentences that are related to the main idea of a paragraph belong in that paragraph. When this is so, we say that a paragraph has *unity*.
    Which paragraph below has unity and which one does not? Put a check next to the one with unity.

    _____The leaves are beginning to turn color. Michael came over to see me yesterday, and I was happy to see him. I need to tell my parents that there are lots of ripe tomatoes in their garden. Today will be a busy day.

    _____The leaves are beginning to turn color. The apples are ripening and falling to the ground. Each day it is getting dark a little earlier, and the weather is cooler. These are signs that summer is turning into fall.

3. A paragraph has a single overall idea that is explained or developed in some way. Understanding how the main idea is supported, or how the ideas of a paragraph are related to each other, is an important part of paragraph comprehension.

In the example below, three reasons support the main idea. See if you can find the main idea. Then find the three reasons which support it. List these reasons below the paragraph.

I know Mr. Forester is a good coach, but I have to admit I am rather frightened of him. Often he yells at us when we're so exhausted we can barely move any more. We just can't give out one hundred percent all the time. Sometimes he acts as though our injuries are just excuses not to play soccer. Worst of all, he hardly ever compliments anyone. I can't tell whether he thinks I am doing a good job or a poor job for the team.

1. _____

2. _____

3. _____

Finding the three reasons in the paragraph should help you understand that a paragraph is a group of sentences that focus on one main idea. All of the sentences work together to develop or explain the main idea. They are related to each other in a number of different ways, but they must be related if the paragraph is to have unity.

Unity

Every paragraph needs to have *unity*. This means that every sentence in the paragraph should be related to the main idea in some clear way.

Your task in this exercise is to see if you can improve the unity of each of the paragraphs below. In each paragraph, there are two sentences that do not fit in with the main idea. First write the main idea of the paragraph on the line above it. Then bracket [ ] the sentences that do not fit in.

The first paragraph has been started for you. The main idea is written in and one of the sentences that does not fit has been bracketed. Find the other one. Then do the same in the other paragraphs.

1.   Why the wolverine is a fierce creature

You may never have seen a wolverine but, take my word for it, the wolverine is a fierce creature. It kills beavers when they go from water to land. [The wolverine is a member of the weasel family.] It raids hunters' traps, and it even raids trappers' camps. Some people think the wolverine looks like a strange raccoon. It not only steals food, but also articles it can't have any use for.

2.   *Noah Webster*

Noah Webster was a very talented person. He wrote a dictionary at a time when there weren't many dictionaries, and when the American language was young. Most people don't like to look up words in dictionaries. He also was a good lawyer and teacher. He was not a politician, but he supported the leaders of our new nation, including George Washington, as he lectured around the country. Even paperback dictionaries today have about 50,000 words in them.

3.   _____

Aunt Martha was having trouble keeping her dog Foxy from chasing cars. She tried training him to stay off the road. Then she tried keeping him in the house. Foxy was a German shepherd. The neighbors were afraid they would hit the dog one day. Foxy was two years old. Finally, Aunt Martha built a large dog pen so Foxy could be outdoors without being a problem to anyone.

Unity

Your job is to improve the unity of each paragraph below. In each paragraph one or two sentences do not fit in with the main idea. Write the main idea of the paragraph on the line above it. Then bracket [ ] the sentence or sentences that do not fit.

1. _____

Zoos have changed a lot in the last seventy-five years. Early in this century the cages in zoos were small and dark. People liked to see strange animals, but they knew the cages were like prison cells. [Children have always loved lions best.] It was easy to feel sorry for the animals. Today, most zoos keep their animals in more natural surroundings. They have more room to roam. Sometimes animals are restrained by wire netting or by ditches they won't cross, instead of by bars. They often have trees and rocks or running water in their compounds. [Zoo keepers pay a lot of money for the animals they put on display.]

2. _____

Many people feel that pro football has turned from sport into a big business. Players seem to care more about the money they make than the team they're playing on. [Coaches and players lose money as well as popularity in a losing season.] I think people prefer baseball to football, anyway. Even the spectators remember the products the players advertise better than the games.

3. _____

If you look carefully at the base of a tree that has been cut down, you can figure out the age of the tree. You do this by counting rings. Rings are made up of bands of light and darker cells. [Oak trees are much taller than maple trees.] The light part of a band is the growth in spring and early summer, while the darker part is the growth of the late summer. [It takes great skill to cut down a tree so that it lands where you want it to land.]

Main Idea

When does one paragraph end and another begin? Remember that a single paragraph should have *one main idea*. When the idea changes, a new paragraph should begin.

The purpose of this exercise is to see if you can tell where a new paragraph should begin. Each set of sentences is really *two* paragraphs. Put the symbol for a new paragraph (¶) before the first sentence of the second paragraph.

1. Larry Curtis raised flowering plants like orchids and rare violets as a hobby. Every morning he watered them, clipped dead leaves, and looked over the flowers. He never had breakfast until he had finished caring for the plants. This often meant that he had to rush to get to the office on time. Imagine Larry's surprise when the president of the Garden Club of America visited him one Saturday. Several of Larry's friends had mentioned the unusualness and the splendor of his plant display. The president lost no time inviting Larry to display his best plants at a special show and to lecture to a group of experts.

2. We open the refrigerator, get out the lemonade, and close the door again. Then, minutes later, we open the refrigerator again to get out the ham, cheese, mustard, and mayonnaise. We don't think about what a small miracle and what a big convenience refrigeration is. What foods do you think we'd eat all year if we didn't have refrigerators? In the eighteenth century, only some people had "iceboxes," the first refrigerators. The food in an icebox was kept cold by ice. The ice came from frozen lakes and ponds in winter and was stored in sawdust in ice houses for summer use. If your family was lucky enough to have an icebox, the ice man arrived several times a week with new blocks of ice that he carried in to your icebox. As the ice melted, water drained out through a hose and had to be collected and emptied. But for all its trouble, an icebox was better than no refrigeration at all.

3. In 1929, a man named Goddard set off an experimental rocket from his aunt's farm in Worcester, Massachusetts. The launching made such a dramatic explosion that police, ambulances, and reporters rushed to the farm expecting an unknown disaster. Goddard was forbidden to set off any more rockets from the farm. Forty years later Apollo 11 was launched from Cape Kennedy. This rocket successfully orbited the earth, and two of its astronauts became the first people to walk on the moon. Apollo 11 was the product of a remarkable growth of technology in a very short period of time.

4. The folding fan is said to have been invented by the Japanese. It was formed on the same principle as bats' wings. A number of sticks shaped like blades are covered with some kind of light material. The blades are held together at the base by a rivet, so the fan can be spread out or closed. To the Japanese, the opening of a fan suggests a happy future. Friends greet each other with a wave of a fan. A bride takes a fan to her husband's house as a gift. Jugglers use the fan, and it is even used by umpires for signals in games.

Topic Sentence

The main idea in a paragraph is usually clearly stated in a sentence called the **topic sentence**. A topic sentence states both the topic (for example, "teeth") and the idea about the topic that is discussed throughout the paragraph. Here are some different topic sentences on the subject of "teeth." Notice that each expresses a different idea about teeth.

Teeth are used for chewing, talking, and whistling.
Some people have more teeth than others.
Teeth need calcium for healthy growth.

Look for the topic sentence — the statement of the main idea — in the paragraph below.

My uncle is a musician who prides himself on playing unusual instruments. His favorite is an old comb, wrapped with a thin layer of tissue paper. He also plays a series of old pottery jugs, filled with water at different levels. Sometimes he gets out the old wash basin and turns it into a kind of bass fiddle. And he never goes anywhere without a couple of kazoos in his pocket!

Topic _____

Topic sentence _____

Most paragraphs, like the one above, begin with the topic sentence so that we get the main idea immediately. In some paragraphs, however, the topic sentence is found in the middle or at the end. If the topic sentence appears in the middle, it often serves to connect two quite different aspects of the main idea. When the topic sentence is at the end, it often pulls together or sums up the discussion of the earlier sentences in the paragraph.

Read the two paragraphs below. One topic sentence is in the middle of the paragraph; the other is at the end. Underline the topic sentence in each one.

1. My brother Arthur was so mad at me that I hid in my closet. When I tried to open the door, I couldn't. It was locked on the outside. I pushed the door and turned the handle every way I could. Then I yelled for Arthur. I even screamed at the top of my lungs. I got so scared! Finally I just sat on my shoes for a long, long time. I got out when my mother came home. There sure is nothing worse than getting locked in your own closet!

2. We had made the sandwiches, and the frisbees, bats, and ball were in the car. Sally was on her way to our house to join us. Still, our parents decided to postpone the picnic. The sky was very cloudy and it was supposed to rain. Looking at the gray sky, my father said that mowing the lawn before the rain started was more important than a picnic.

Topic Sentence

Read each paragraph below. Find the topic sentence. Put brackets [ ] around it. On the line above the paragraph put a title that expresses the main idea.

1. _____

Historians believe that the tribal war began in 1567 and ended in 1570. Tribes from the region of Simala joined together under the leadership of Rimbolu. They needed to help each other fight off the attacks of the Gumbi tribes. In the beginning it seemed as if neither side had superior manpower or organization. Now and then over the next three years, news of skirmishes between the tribes in the two regions reached the outside world. When no further reports of victories or losses came from the jungle, everyone figured the war was over.

2. _____

At first Judy didn't like the kids in her cabin] She thought her counselor was bossy. Soon she got involved in some activities she enjoyed. She liked the water skiing and canoeing the best. Betsy, one of the girls in her cabin, became her best friend. Even her counselor didn't seem so bad. By the end of the first week, she was having such fun that she knew she wouldn't want to go home when her month at camp was over.

3. _____

Have you ever picked up a box of matches with the label "safety matches"? A safety match is safe because it will light only when it is struck on a specially prepared surface. With other matches, all the chemicals needed to light the match are included in the match head. With safety matches, one of the chemicals (red phosphorous) is painted on the striking surface. The match will not light unless it is rubbed on this particular kind of striking area.

4. _____

Have you ever walked through the woods and found a stone wall weaving among the trees? I have, and I have wondered why anyone would bother to build a stone wall going through the woods. As it turns out, stone walls were put up by early farmers to mark the boundaries of their fields and farmland. Stone walls that are now in the woods originally surrounded cleared pasture land and tended fields. The time came when no one mowed the fields. Brush crept in, and then trees. Nature reclaimed her own territory, even though the walls remained.

Topic Sentence

Some paragraphs do not have a topic sentence. Instead, they are written in such a way that the main idea of the paragraph becomes clear from the whole discussion. A paragraph without a topic sentence often lists events in the order they occur, or tells a story. Such paragraphs are often called *narrative* paragraphs.

The paragraphs below do not have topic sentences. Read each one. Then write the main idea of the paragraph on the line below it.

1. Most of the firefighters awoke when the first bolts of thunder and lightning struck. The sound was so intense that they could tell that this would be a day of trouble. Sure enough, the phone rang and five minutes later the fire alarm sounded. Lightning had struck the church on West Avenue. No sooner had the first fire engine crew left than the alarm sounded again, this time because a tree had fallen across electric wires on Chestnut Street. Twice more in the course of the morning a fire truck left the firehouse in the rain and wind. The storm was intense, but luckily for the tired firefighters it was also short-lived.

_____

2. In the 1840s a large number of immigrants came to America from Scandinavia. In the 1840s and 1850s the wave of immigration spread so that new peoples were arriving from all over northern and western Europe — Great Britain, Germany, Ireland, and other countries. Both groups of immigrants left homelands because of problems they encountered there — potato famines, revolutions, or shortages of land that could be farmed. They also looked to America for the answers to their dreams. Settling in to their new lives took decades, a period interrupted by the start of the Civil War in 1861.

_____

3. Sally Fleming started swimming in the pool at the YMCA when she was three years old. She competed in swimming events throughout the state until she had graduated from high school. Then she decided that it was long-distance swimming that mattered. First she swam across various lakes, then across harbors along the coast. At last she was ready to tackle the English Channel. On her first try she gave up, beaten by the fog and rain and the currents. Her second try was successful.

_____

Phrasing Topics

The exercise below will give you practice finding and stating the main idea found in a topic sentence. You need to look for the words that tell you not only the *topic*, but also *the idea about the topic*. To do this exercise write the main idea of the sentence as a short phrase. Here is an example on the topic of acrobats:

Acrobats begin their training as young children for several reasons.

Phrase: Why acrobats begin training as young children.

The phrase should express the idea that will be discussed through the whole paragraph.

For each topic sentence, write a short phrase that expresses the main idea on the line below the sentence.

1. A good way to earn money during the school year is by being a newspaper carrier.

   _____

2. Aunt Edith spends her days in very peculiar ways.

   _____

3. Why does it cost so much to send a single, thin letter by mail?

   _____

4. German shepherds do important jobs for people, such as working as guard dogs or seeing-eye dogs.

   _____

5. Different constellations of stars can be seen in the sky in different parts of the world.

   _____

6. If you have to wear eyeglasses, try to choose a style that suits the shape of your face.

   _____

7. Jumping rope is an activity that is always popular with children.

   _____

Phrasing Topics

For each topic sentence write a short phrase that expresses the main idea on the line below the sentence. Put a star after these directions to show that you have read them.

1. I spent a wonderful day at the Johnsons' farm helping with the haying.

   _____

2. Wait until you hear what happened the day Uncle Phil took the car to do errands but forgot his driving glasses.

   _____

3. These days reading road maps requires great skill.

   _____

4. Historians argue about the most important causes of the Civil War.

   _____

5. A recent survey tells us how much money the average fourteen-year-old spends in a year.

   _____

6. There are many advantages to being left-handed, though most right-handers aren't aware of them.

   _____

7. As any expert on nutrition will tell you, eating too much sugar is quite harmful to your body.

   _____

8. Most people in the United States don't get as much exercise as they need for healthy bodies.

   _____

9. Young people go to college for a number of different reasons, not just to get an education.

   _____

10. People have very different ideas about what makes a good vacation.

   _____

Signal Words

Shifts in thought or sequences of ideas are usually connected by signal words or phrases. A signal word, like a traffic signal, gives you an indication of a change. A red light is a signal to stop, while a green light is a signal to go. Because signal words direct your attention to new ideas, they help present ideas in a clear and organized fashion.

Some signal words present sequences of ideas of equal importance. Here are examples: first, second, third; one ____, a second ____; some ____, other ____, still other. Other signal words are used to clarify the relationship between ideas. Here are some examples:

Time order: first; then; next; finally
Comparison: on the other hand; however
Cause-Effect: as a result; therefore

Read the following paragraph, looking for signal words. You should be able to find *five* signal words. Underline each one.

Elaine borrowed her uncle's pick-up truck to help Bud move to his new apartment in Chester. First they had to remove the cinder blocks that were in the truck already. Next they had to borrow old blankets from Elaine's aunt and parents. Then they started off on the highway to Woroville. They packed up the truck in short order. But halfway to Chester, the truck sputtered and stopped. They had run out of gas. Finally, after a walk to the nearest gas station, they reached the apartment in Chester before dark.

The exercise that follows will make you think about the kind of relationship different signal words indicate. Read the short sentences and the signal words or phrases that follow. Then write a sentence which gives the reader an idea of what to expect from that particular signal word. The first one has been done for you.

1. I know you love cats. *However,*   dogs make friendlier pets. _____

2. Guido broke five of the red glasses. *As a result,* _____

   _____

3. Mr. Lesko backed the car out of the garage. *Then* _____

   _____

4. Myrna has lots of hobbies. *For example,* _____

   _____

5. Some of the birds eat sunflower seeds. *Others* _____

   _____

Signal Words

Read each paragraph. Then follow the directions given below it.

1.   One day the Watkins discovered that their dog had fleas — not just a few fleas, but lots of fleas. Marty and Bill decided to see if fleas could really jump. First, while Mr. Watkins was getting ready to bathe the dog, they each caught a flea on the dog. Then, holding the fleas tightly between two fingers, they ran to the bathtub and let the fleas loose. Next, as the fleas started leaping all over, they laughed and argued. Soon the boys had trouble keeping track of where the fleas were. Suddenly both fleas were gone. The boys felt itchy just thinking that the fleas might be in their hair.

First find and circle the signal words. Then beside each signal word, write what happened at that point. From your list we will be able to see the steps of the Watkins boys' adventure.

First _____

Then   _____

Next _____

Soon _____

Suddenly _____

2.   Uncle Mario had some unusual friends. One was a trainer of circus dogs. Mario saw him only when the circus came to town. Another was an inventor. She had come up with a new design for bottle tops that had made her wealthy, yet she continued to live in a ramshackle barn and eat only baked beans for dinner. Still another, a dealer in antique cars, called himself Dandy. He took Mario on trips around the country as he delivered or picked up cars. They collected postcards as they traveled.

The three signal words or phrases are: _____

_____

The examples that follow the signal words are: _____

_____

_____

Signal Words

Read each paragraph. Then follow the directions given below it.

1. Hunting developed from a necessity to a sport in America. The first settlers in America found plenty of wild game. At first they needed to hunt to survive. They lived on deer and wild turkey. Then, as they prospered and had more free time, hunting as a sport became popular. Any person who owned a gun could hunt. Soon big game, such as the buffalo and antelope, became scarce because they had been killed in such great numbers. After that, sportspersons and naturalists worked to pass game laws that would prevent too much killing. The laws set the hunting seasons and the game limits.

Find and circle the signal words. Then in the space below, list the four steps in the events that are pointed out by the signal words.

_____

_____

_____

2. Many strange bicycles were invented before a machine similar to the bicycle we use today was developed. First a very basic bicycle called the *dandyhorse* was invented. It consisted of two wheels attached to a wooden bar. The rider straddled the bar and pushed the ground with his feet to make the bicycle move forward. Later, the *boneshaker* was invented. It probably did shake one's bones to ride it because it had two wooden wheels with iron tires. It also had pedals on the front wheel axle, like our present tricycles. Still later, the *ordinary* was invented. Its wheel had solid rubber tires. The front wheel was larger and heavier than the rear wheel, causing the bike to be unstable. People were known to fall over the front handlebars.

1. Circle the signal words that point to the three examples. Underline the names of the bicycles discussed.

2. Explain how the three bicycles were different.

_____

_____

Examples

An example is an item that is a part of or a representative of a group. Examples of the group "vegetable" include carrots, beans, and peas. Maui and Tahiti are examples of islands in the Pacific Ocean.

Examples are commonly used to make a general idea clear and concrete. They are helpful to the reader.

In each of the following paragraphs underline the main idea. Then list the examples that are given in the paragraph. The first one has been started.

1. Mr. and Mrs. Hardy were very upset with their son Fred because it seemed to them that he ate almost nothing but junk food. He'd start off his day with two doughnuts and a cup of coffee. For lunch he'd eat a pizza or some french fries at one of the fast-food stores in town. He'd arrive home at five o'clock so hungry that he'd have a soda or two and a bag of potato chips before dinner. Then he wouldn't be hungry enough to eat a decent dinner at 6 o'clock, so by 9 o'clock he would make himself a big hot-fudge sundae.

    Examples: a. doughnuts and coffee

    b.

    c.

    d.

2. Professor Smile had taught biology for so many years that he could tell certain types of students after the first few days of class. Some students identified themselves by the part of the classroom they chose to sit in. The students who sat in the back were usually the laziest or least interested. On the other hand, the students who sat in the front row were either eager and ambitious or near-sighted. The near-sighted type was easy to sort out because they wore glasses. In addition, he thought that the students who sat near the windows were either daydreamers or naturalists.

    Examples: (Give positions in the classroom and characteristics.)

    a.

    b.

    c.

Examples

Read each paragraph. Underline the topic sentence. List the examples of the main idea that are given in the paragraph. The first one has been started for you. Finish the first paragraph. Then go on to the second.

1. The grocery bag I was carrying was heavy and awkward. <u>Before I reached the car, the bottom of the bag ripped and Andrea's groceries ended up all over the sidewalk.</u> The gallon of milk landed on the tomatoes. The pickle jar broke in half. Most of the eggs splattered on the sidewalk, and mayonnaise oozed over everything. The worst part was that apples rolled away in all directions because I felt too embarrassed to chase after them.

Examples:

a.

b.

c.

d.

e.

f.

2. I like to babysit for most of the families that call me, but some children are so impossible or unpleasant that I'd rather sit at home bored than take care of them. Some babies cry all the time, even when I rock them. Then there are kids like the Bowen twins, who throw their food and toys all over the house. But most exhausting of all are children like the MacLeans, who fight and yell at each other all the time. I cannot get them to stop. So the next time Mr. MacLean calls, I will tell him I'm studying for a test.

Examples:

a.

b.

c.

3. Telling time is not just a matter of learning to read the face of a clock or watch. Nature has its own methods for reminding us about time. Time is marked by the passage of seasons. We tell time by the shifts from night to day and by the passage of the sun in the sky. We even mark time by the needs of our own bodies. Hunger and sleep, for instance, remind us of the time of day or night.

Examples:

a.

b.

c.

Support for the Main Idea

The paragraph is structurally suited to presenting an idea, opinion, or belief, and then facts, examples, or reasons to explain and support the initial idea. You have already seen how examples can clarify the point of a paragraph. Reasons and other forms of support have a similiar purpose. The best way to find these reasons or points of support for a main idea is to state the main idea and then ask the question, "Why?" The answers are the points used to explain and support the main idea. The paragraph below is an example. Notice that the main idea is in the first sentence: Ben Brady hates camping. As you read the paragraph, think about *why* he dislikes camping. List the four reasons below the paragraph.

   Ben Brady hates camping. First, he doesn't like hiking to the campsite with a heavy backpack chafing his shoulders, particularly in hot weather. Second, he finds unpacking and repacking the equipment boring. It is worse than housekeeping in his apartment. In addition, he finds sleeping on the ground most uncomfortable, even using an air mattress. Most of all, though, he is bothered by the insects that arrive at mealtime and bedtime. Swatting flies leaves him so grouchy that he feels out of sorts with himself.

   Reasons that Ben Brady hates camping:

   a.

   b.

   c.

   d.

Now find the reasons that explain why a quaking bog is the strangest of all the types of wetland.

   Swamps, marshes, and bogs are called wetlands. The strangest of all of these wetlands is the quaking bog. Standing at the edge of the bog, you will see an area that is generally flat and covered with low plants and bushes. The ground looks solid, but when you walk on it, the ground shifts, sending waves outward. Bushes a distance away shake, and your feet get wet. The true floor of the bog may be five to twenty feet below. You are actually standing on the plant layer floating on the surface of the quaking bog.

   Why a quaking bog is strange:

   a.

   b.

Support for the Main Idea

The purpose of this exercise is to give you practice finding the points an author uses to support the main idea. First find the topic sentence. Express the main idea as a phrase and write it next to roman numeral I. Next find the points that explain and support the main idea. Write these as phrases next to capital letters A, B, and so on. The first one has been started for you.

Some people like to watch baseball games, and some don't. Still, whether we know it or not, we all use the language of baseball in our everyday speech. For example, you'll hear a person say, "He's way out in left field." Whoever it is does not understand the reality of a situation. Sometimes you also hear the expression, "She threw me a curve." The speaker is using the term "curve (ball)" to mean an unexpected problem. A third phrase you hear now and then is "born with two strikes against him." Since with three strikes you're out, a person born with two strikes has a lot going against him or her from the start.

    I. Baseball language in everyday speech

       A. "Way out in left field"
       B.
       C.

Bats use their sonar systems to hunt for food at night. Did you know that bats feed at night on almost every kind of food birds feed on during the day? Some bats feed on insects. Others eat fruit or pollen or even nectar from night-blooming flowers. One particular kind, the vampire bat, drains small amounts of blood from large animals. Another kind captures roosting birds or even other bats. Like the hawk, this type is a carnivore.

    I. A.
       B.
       C.
       D.

If it strikes you that children are becoming spoiled by the thousands of toys available to them, you should notice the games and toys that don't bore them after a day or two. Some are games that require no equipment — hide-and-seek, for example. Others are activities invented from the simplest odds and ends — clubhouses, home-made vehicles, and the like. Still others are toys similar to the ones their grandparents played with. These include marbles, balls, rag dolls, and blocks.

    I.
       A.
       B.
       C.

Support for the Main Idea

Read each paragraph below. Underline the main idea. Make an outline of the main idea and supporting points, as you have done on the previous exercises. This time it is up to you to structure your own outline.

When the first explorers gave the natives on the islands gifts, the natives thought their visitors were kind and generous people. In fact, however, the explorers caused a great deal of trouble. For one thing, the natives argued and fought over who deserved the beads and brightly colored shirts. Family turned against family as the natives competed for the attention of the visitors. In addition, the natives did not truly understand what these men said to them; neither could they read or write the visitors' language. So they did not realize that they had given away their island for a few trinkets and pieces of pretty clothing. And then, at last, when a few of their people had died from weapons that spouted fire and noise and metal, the natives realized that their visitors were not leaving.

Dieticians tell us that most of us eat too much sugar for our own good. Their first concern is our health. We eat doughnuts and sugared fruit juices for breakfast, and we feel full and satisfied. Yet the sugar gives us empty calories — no vitamins, no minerals, and no protein. So in the long run the health of our bodies is threatened or damaged. In addition, while we may get a spurt of quick energy from ice cream cones and sodas, this sort of energy runs out quickly, leaving us tired and cranky. The highs and lows of our energy levels in turn affect how much work we can do well in a day, physically, or mentally. Shifts in energy and disposition are dieticians' second concern.

Support for the Main Idea

This is a writing exercise. You will start it on this sheet, but you will need to finish on a separate sheet of paper. The purpose is to give you practice supporting a main idea when you write a paragraph.

Here is the topic sentence of your paragraph:

You can't always believe advertisements.

First, think of three points that support this idea. List them below.

1. _____

_____

2. _____

_____

3. _____

Next, check your statements to make sure that they really do support the main idea. For example, this sentence does *not* support the main idea: "There are more advertisements on television than on radio." If you have listed any points that do not clearly support the main idea, change them now.

Finally, using a separate piece of paper, write out your paragraph, starting with the topic sentence. Use signal words to show where your new points are. Add sentences that help the reader understand your points.

Once you have revised your paragraph so that it is a clear and complete explanation of your points, you will probably find writing other paragraphs of this type less difficult. Here are several topic sentences. Choose one and, following the same directions as above, write a second paragraph building support for the main idea.

Our society is a wasteful one.

Young adults need to be given responsibilities.

Cause-Effect

Apart from examples and explanations, ideas in a paragraph can be related to each other in a number of different ways. A cause-effect relationship is one of these ways.

In a cause-effect paragraph, one situation causes or results from another. For example, Arthur's ten-speed bike has a bent front wheel. A cause-effect paragraph could explain how the front wheel was damaged or what happened as a result of the damage. Sometimes a cause-effect paragraph will present a chain of events that are sequences of causes and effects. The paragraph that follows is an example.

   As Arthur was riding down Harvest Avenue, a yellow delivery truck sped through an intersection, ignoring the stop sign. He swerved to miss the truck, skidded in the dirt, and slid into a brick wall. When he got himself up, he realized that his leg was badly scraped, but even worse, his front wheel was so badly bent that he couldn't even ride the bike home.

Sometimes a cause-effect paragraph will give a number of causes or a number of effects of a situation. Here is an example.

   We knew that there were often brutal fights between the Eagles and the White Stars, but no one expected such a severe battle. There were several reasons for the explosion. First of all, the teams were competing for popularity in the northwest. Second, Jean Delane put an elbow into Michael Tilbault's face as he skated by in the warm-ups. A collision between these two players later in the game renewed their anger. Unfortunately, the last reason is that the fans were egging the fighters on. Sticks and gloves flew across the ice. Team loyalty involved one player after another. So many players were either injured or suspended from the game that the game itself had to be cancelled.

List the *causes* of the fight below. How many causes were there? _____

_____

_____

What was the *effect* of the fight? _____

_____

_____

Cause-Effect

Read the paragraphs and answer the questions.

In the year 1848 a man named John Sutter was building a sawmill in California. His helper, James Marshall, noticed flakes of yellow metal mixed with the gravel from the stream. News of the presence of this yellow metal caused a great stir throughout the United States. Thousands of people left their homes and headed toward California in 1849. On the way, many died from starvation or the desert heat. Some turned back because the trip was so difficult. Many of the people who made it to California ended up having arguments and fights over the use and ownership of land. A few people grew rich very rapidly. Why did the yellow metal cause such a stir? It was gold!

In this paragraph, one cause (the discovery of gold) had a number of effects. What were they? List four.

1. _____

2. _____

3. _____

4. _____

Every time people had dinner with the Sullivans, they felt as though they had had a gigantic Thanksgiving meal. Mr. and Mrs. Sullivan put dish after dish of good food on the table and kept begging their guests to eat more. Maybe the reason for this is that both Mr. and Mrs. Sullivan grew up in families that never had enough to eat. Food, and lots of it, was a very real sign of health and happiness to them.

What caused Mr. and Mrs. Sullivan to serve large meals? _____

_____

_____

You might think that your eating habits are controlled by what tastes good to you, but there are other matters that condition you to prefer certain foods. Your family background is one influence. Most of us like to eat foods we are familiar with and foods that have pleasant associations for us. In addition, our body seems to play a role in guiding us to eat foods that it needs. Too many sugary foods, for example, are sickening, so we turn to a glass of milk and toast for a snack.

List two causes of our food preferences. _____

_____

Time Order

When a paragraph presents events with a concern for the order in which they occurred, we say that the sentences are related by **time order**. The focus can be on events that happened **before, after,** or **at the same time** as another event. The ideas in the following paragraph are related because they form a sequence.

1. Eight years ago, Anne Murphy and I graduated from college. Anne had always dreamed of becoming a surgeon, so she went to medical school. When she finished her training there, she became an intern in a hospital in New York. For two years after that she was a resident in surgery in a hospital in Boston. The next thing I heard, she had moved to Chicago. She was a surgeon on the staff of the Michael Reese Hospital. She has come a long way in eight years. I'm still working at the same job.

List the events after Anne's graduation.

1.

2.

3.

4.

2. Do you remember Mr. Lenz, the janitor at school? He was a soft-spoken man who liked to tell us about his adventures as a spy. I remember one story he told about being held captive in a desert cabin until he tricked his captors into letting him go. I don't think any of us believed his stories. I didn't, until my father showed me an article printed when Mr. Lenz retired. I read that Mr. Lenz won many sharp-shooting competitions as a youngster. He graduated from college with honors, majoring in economics. He fought in World War II until he was seriously wounded. He received a Purple Heart for bravery in action. Then he worked for the government for many years. Perhaps he really was a spy — the article didn't say. Still, I was impressed with the active and adventurous life Mr. Lenz had led.

Number Mr. Lenz's activities so that they are in correct time order.

_____ soldier   _____ sharp-shooting champion

_____ retirement   _____ college student

_____ janitor   _____ spy

Time Order

The sentences in these paragraphs are *not* in order. Number them so that they are presented in the order in which they happened. Read all the sentences before you begin numbering them. The first sentence has been marked for you.

Paragraph 1:

___1___ Harold was an ambitious noble who decided to bring order to the land by convincing the tribes in the south to work together instead of fighting among themselves.

_____ Next, having shown the neighboring chiefs the value of working together, Harold invited them all to his castle to learn the pleasures of social gatherings.

_____ It was a great victory when Harold was crowned king in 926.

_____ First he had to subdue all feuding tribes whose land bordered his own.

_____ While they were gathered peacefully, he encouraged the tribal chiefs to talk out their differences and treat each other with respect.

_____ Then from 919 to 923 he used his own power and the support of neighboring tribes, newly conquered, to battle against rebellious chiefs from the north and the west.

Paragraph 2:

_____ Henry Ford, an inventor of the "horseless carriage," spent many years doing other things before he produced the first Model A car.

_____ When he was sixteen he went to Detroit and worked for five years as a helper in an engine shop.

_____ He was born in 1863 in Dearborn, Michigan, the son of a farmer.

_____ After five years, he returned to Detroit, and while he worked for a company as an engineer and machinist, he also started building a "horseless carriage" in a workshop in his backyard.

_____ In 1886 he returned to the farm and worked at a number of jobs — running a sawmill, building farm engines, and repairing machinery.

_____ As a young boy, he worked hard on the farm, but he also developed a strong interest in machinery.

Comparison

The purpose of some paragraphs is to show similarities and differences between two or more things. The relationship between the ideas, therefore, is one of **comparison**. Sometimes the focus of a paragraph of comparison is the similarities; sometimes it is the differences. However, in every paragraph of comparison you should make sure you understand what is being compared and exactly what the similarities and differences are.

The following paragraph is a comparison. Does it focus primarily on similarities or differences?

Louisa and Denise set off together to climb Mt. Hadden. The two had been good friends for years, and they were sure they would make a good team. When they got back, though, they both had learned how different the two of them were. Louisa is the kind of person who takes life easy, while Denise is eager and energetic. On the trip, Louisa's idea of a good morning was to sleep late, eat breakfast slowly, and start to climb by 9 o'clock. Denise was out of bed and ready to go by 7. Their climbing was just as different. Louisa was yards behind Denise, always ready to stop for a rest. They're still good friends, but they probably won't climb together again.

What similarities between Louisa and Denise are mentioned? _____

_____

_____

How are the two women different? _____

_____

_____

_____

Butterflies and kites give us similar kinds of pleasure. Both are colorful, often unusual in their design. Both flutter or fly quietly, dipping and darting with small changes in the wind. It is the combination of color, design, and movement that makes us notice them particularly.

What two things are compared in this paragraph? _____

_____

List the similarities or differences. _____

_____

Comparison

Read each paragraph. Then answer the questions below.

When an athlete in America wins a contest, he or she may receive a ribbon or a school letter or a medal. This isn't what happens everywhere. The national sport of Spain is bullfighting; the matador is the star athlete in this type of contest. If a matador is able to kill his bull, he walks around the ring and people throw hats and coins to him. If the matador has done well, he is given one ear from the bull he killed. If he has done a very good job, he is given one ear and the tail. That kind of recognition for a job well done is very different from what we are used to in America.

1. What two things are being compared in this paragraph? _____

_____

2. How are the two things different? _____

_____

While his parents and grandparents were talking, Ron got out an album of old family pictures. He came upon a picture of a young woman who looked as though she were about to go swimming. But she had on a black dress and stockings of some kind and a funny hat. He asked his grandmother who the woman in the picture was, and why she was standing in the water with all those clothes on. His grandmother told him that the picture was of his great grandmother and that she was going swimming. ''Going swimming in those clothes!'' he thought. All he could think of was his sister and her friends and the kinds of bathing suits that they wore now. How different the generations were!

1. What two things is Ron comparing in his mind? _____

_____

2. List the details that show the differences. _____

_____

_____

Definition

A paragraph can be written in order to clarify the meaning of a word or phrase. This kind of writing is called a paragraph of **definition**.

Paragraphs of definition are likely to use some of the other types of relationships we have seen in order to make the meaning clear. Sometimes examples are given. Sometimes an incident is related or a history reviewed, using time order. In the paragraph below you will notice that the meaning of several words is made clear. The author clarifies the different meanings of somewhat similar words by comparing them to each other.

Here is an example of a paragraph of definition:

Your parents probably ask you to take out the garbage. And I'll bet your family talks about taking the garbage to the dump or wonders when the garbage collector is coming. We use the word garbage when we talk about all the stuff we throw away. But garbage is really the waste material from your kitchen — potato peels, egg shells, and so forth. When you throw out waste paper, bottles, cans, boxes, or rags you're throwing out rubbish. A third type of waste material is what is left from burning coal or wood: these are ashes. The general word for all three kinds of waste materials is refuse. Refuse is everything we throw out. Your parents may be right when they ask you to take the garbage out, but if you're going to the dump, you're probably getting rid of refuse.

1. Four words are defined in this paragraph. What are they? _____

    _____

2. This paragraph uses examples to make the meaning clear. Give an example of

    garbage:_____ Give an example of rubbish:_____

3. Explain how rubbish is different from refuse._____

    _____

    _____

    _____

Definition

Read the paragraphs below. Then answer the questions that follow them.

Most people think a lake is different from a pond because it is a larger body of water. Biologists, however, don't distinguish a lake from a pond because of a difference in size. To them, the difference is the depth of the water. A pond is a body of water so shallow that light shines through to the bottom. A lake, on the other hand, has depths that are always dark.

1. What two words are defined here? _____

2. The two words are clarified by use of a comparison. How are the two different to a

   biologist? _____

   _____

3. Write down two signal words or phrases found in this paragraph. _____

   _____

Historically, many wars have been fought over freedom. But freedom has meant different things to different people. The American revolution was fought mostly for political or national freedom. People in the colonies did not want to be governed by Great Britain. They wanted the freedom to govern themselves. In contrast, the French revolution that came a little later was fought for personal freedom and dignity. The common people would no longer put up with the way they had been treated by the king and the upper classes.

1. The point of this paragraph is to make clear the meaning of two types of freedom. What are they? _____

   _____

   How are they different? _____

   _____

2. The first sentence is not the topic sentence. Which sentence is the topic sentence? Underline it.

Relationships

The purpose of these writing exercises is to give you practice writing particular types of paragraphs. Make sure you understand how the sentences in the paragraph must relate to each other before you start writing. Use separate pieces of paper; follow your teacher's instructions.

Exercise 1:

Write a paragraph of **comparison**. The topic sentence is: Baseball and softball are very much alike.

Exercise 2:

Write a paragraph of **cause and effect**. The topic sentence is: Guess what happened when our dog knocked over the ladder Mr. Brown was standing on.

Exercise 3:

Write a paragraph based on **time order**. The topic sentence is: I'll never do that again!

Exercise 4:

Write a paragraph giving **examples** or supporting the idea with a list of reasons. The topic sentence is: My little sister has found lots of uses for a baseball bat. (You may use fishing rod or hockey stick instead.)

Exercise 5:

Write a paragraph of **definition**. The topic sentence is: My parents and teachers think school means one thing, but I think it means something quite different.

Exercise 6:

Use both **comparison** and **examples** in writing your paragraph this time. The topic sentence is: Many people think different colors express different feelings.

Practice

Read the paragraph. Then answer the questions below.

One of the main jobs of the Federal Bureau of Investigation (the FBI) is to help local law enforcement agencies. The FBI runs a laboratory equipped with the latest scientific crime detection equipment. First, the FBI is able to help local law agencies by examining all kinds of material scientifically — for example, documents, hair, and soil. In addition, the FBI keeps files of information such as types of paint and tire markings. Using these files, an agent sometimes finds a small piece of evidence that will trap a criminal. For example, it is possible to examine a typewritten note and tell what kind of typewriter typed it. After examining the evidence local agencies have sent them, FBI experts will also help by testifying in court about their findings.

1. What is the main idea of this paragraph? _____

    _____

2. Most of the paragraph gives an explanation of the main idea. There are three main supporting points. List them below.

    1. _____

    2. _____

    3. _____

3. The paragraph also gives examples. Find an example of the type of materials the experts

    examine: _____

    Find an example of the type of information kept on file: _____

    _____

    Find an example of a small piece of evidence that could trap a criminal: _____

    _____

4. Find two signal words or phrases used in the paragraph: _____

    _____

Practice

Read the following paragraph. Then answer the questions.

A fable is a fanciful story, very much like a myth. It is not true. It is based on folklore and legend and sometimes the supernatural. In fables animals are able to talk, for example. A fox is able to ask a crow to drop him grapes from a tree. People all over the world have enjoyed fables for centuries. Fables told over the years have been collected and recorded in books. Why have fables been so popular? First, some fables were used to explain mysterious facts of nature, such as what thunder is or why caves echo. Second, most fables have a moral to the story. The moral reminds people about some important lesson that life teaches. "Slow and steady wins the race" is the moral of one fable, for example. Finally, people of all ages enjoy the make-believe world of fables, much as they have always enjoyed fairy tales.

1. This paragraph contains a definition. Which word is defined? _____

2. Examples are given in three places in the paragraph. Underline the examples.

3. At the beginning and at the end of the paragraph a comparison is used to show a

   similarity. What two things are compared to a fable? _____

   _____

4. Write down two signal words used in the paragraph. _____

   _____

5. List two of the reasons given to explain why fables are popular. _____

   _____

   _____

   _____

   _____

Practice

Read the paragraph. Then answer the questions below.

There are a number of strange similarities in the deaths of Abraham Lincoln and John F. Kennedy, too many to be brushed off lightly. First, Lincoln was elected president in 1860, and one hundred years later, in 1960, Kennedy was elected president. Second, the two men were also born one hundred years apart, and so were their assassins, John Wilkes Booth and Lee Harvey Oswald. Third, some of the details of the assassinations are the same. Both men were assassinated from behind. Both were also killed in the presence of their wives. Finally, and perhaps the strangest coincidence of all, Kennedy's secretary, whose name was Lincoln, advised him not to go to Dallas, where he was shot. Similarly, Lincoln's secretary, whose name was Kennedy, advised him not to go to the Ford Theatre, where he was shot.

1. Is the relationship of ideas in this paragraph time order, cause-effect or comparison?

   _____

2. Underline the topic sentence. Circle the word in the topic sentence that makes the relationship you chose above clear.

3. List four signal words used to point out the supporting points.

   _____   _____   _____   _____

4. Now list the four points that support the main idea.

   a._____

   b._____

   c._____

   d._____

Practice

The following paragraph contains four sentences that do not belong, thus ruining the unity of the paragraph. Read the whole paragraph, and then cross out these four sentences. Decide what the main idea of the paragraph is. State this idea as a phrase that serves as the title of the paragraph. Put the title on the line.

_____

Jujitsu, the Japanese art of fighting without weapons, was first used many centuries ago. Jujitsu is practiced in a room called a *doju*. No one is sure how jujitsu first got started. The rank of contestants in jujitsu is shown by the color of the belt. The earliest record of jujitsu dates back to 230 B.C. At this time, jujitsu was used in a contest of strength called the tournament of *chikura-kouraba*, not as a means of fighting. Jujitsu makes use not only of the body, but also the mind. From the twelfth century until about the seventeenth century, Japanese warriors fought in close contact with spears and swords; sometimes they had to use bare hands. During this time the common people had to develop a method of barehanded fighting because they were not allowed to carry swords. Japanese wrestling is called *sumo*. Gradually, over the years, the Japanese discovered better and better ways of using their hands, fingers, elbows, knees, and feet to poke, hit, and drop an opponent.

1. Is the method of presenting information in this paragraph comparison, time order, or examples? (Choose one.)

_____

2. How do you know? _____

_____

Following Directions

Use a separate piece of paper to follow this set of directions.

Tom Sellins lives in an apartment with his wife, Bertha Sellins, and their two children, Jean, who is nine, and Chris, who is five. Over the past four years, they have had two dogs and a cat whose names are Nina, Pinta, and Santa Maria. Though they are crowded in their apartment, they have lived there for seven years.

1. Print your name in about the middle of your paper.
2. If you know Mr. Sellins' first name, circle your last name. Otherwise, circle your first name.
3. If the apartment was less crowded when the Sellinses first moved in, draw a squiggly line from your first name to the top left corner. If it was more crowded, draw a squiggly line under your name. It is was just as crowded then as it is now, draw a squiggly line from your last name to the lower left corner.
4. If Jean is a boy and Chris is a girl, draw a square in the top right corner. If Jean is a girl and Chris is a boy, draw a square in the lower right corner. If you don't have enough information to tell, draw a square in the lower left corner.
5. The dogs' names are Nina and Pinta. If the cat's name is not Santa Maria, draw a heart over your last name. If the cat's name is not Pinta, draw a heart in the upper right corner.
6. If the Sellinses are planning to move, draw an arrow from the heart to the square. If the Sellinses are not planning to move, draw an arrow from your last name to the heart. If you can't tell, draw an arrow from your last name to the lower right corner.

Following Directions

Put your name in the lower left-hand corner of a separate sheet of paper. Then follow this set of directions.

Mrs. Smart left her husband the following directions so that he could meet her at their son's League Championship baseball game. Mr. Smart can follow directions better if he has a map. Make a map for him, showing everything mentioned in the directions. If you make any mistakes, he might not get there! Start by drawing the Smart's house in the lower right-hand corner of your paper. North is toward the top of the page; south is toward the bottom.

Go north on Elm Street until you come to Long Lake, on your left. After you pass the lake, take a left turn on East Street, heading west. You will pass a gas station on your left, and then three large pine trees on your right. After the pine trees, turn right, heading north on Route 225. You will go through three stoplights about two miles apart. After the fourth stoplight, turn left on Union Road. After only a few yards, turn right on Route 6. You will pass two white houses on your left and then two white houses on your right. The next house on the right is yellow. Take the driveway across the road from the yellow house. The baseball field is at the end of this driveway. See you there!

Following Directions

Use a separate sheet of paper to follow this set of directions.

Geraldine Webb, who is twenty-five years old, lives with her father, her uncle, and her brother. Her uncle, Kevin Webb, is older than her father, but he drives a racy sports car. Her brother Ralph is two years younger than she is; he drives an old, rusted-out jeep. Her father is sixty-one and still drives the old Cadillac he bought twenty years ago.

a. Print your name in about the middle of the paper.

b. If Geraldine is the youngest of the four family members, draw a squiggly line under your name. Otherwise, circle your name.

c. If Kevin is over sixty-one years old, draw a square in the top right-hand corner. If not, draw a triangle there.

d. If the man who drives the Cadillac is the younger brother of the man who drives the jeep, draw a line from your first name to the lower left corner. Otherwise, draw a line from your last name to the lower right corner.

e. If Ralph is twenty-three years old, draw a heart in the top left corner. Otherwise, draw a circle there.

f. If the Cadillac is older than Geraldine, draw a heart under your last name. Otherwise, draw a star over your last name.

g. If we know that every member of the family has a car, write *yes* at the bottom of your paper in about the center. Otherwise, write *no* there.

Following Directions

Use a separate sheet of paper to follow this set of directions.

Valerie Marshall has a busy day coming up. At 9:45 this morning she has to pick up some books at the printer and take them to a designer. She has a committee meeting at the business library at 11:00 and a lunch appointment with her assistant at 12:30. She changed her dentist appointment from 2:00 to 1:45 because she has to pick up her daughter, Sue, at school to go to a squash match at 2:30. Sue has a ride home at 4 o'clock, but Mrs. Marshall has to pick Tim up at school then. She plans to go to the market on her way home. She wants to have a simple dinner because she and her husband have to leave for a meeting at 7 o'clock.

a. Draw a circle in the top right hand corner if there is an hour and a half between the time Mrs. Marshall picks up the books and her library meeting. If there isn't an hour and a half, put a check (✔) in the bottom left corner.

b. Draw a square in the lower left corner if Mrs. Marshall has an hour and a half to have lunch with her assistant. If she doesn't have an hour and a half, put a check there.

c. Draw a triangle in the lower right corner if Mrs. Marshall will go to the market soon after 4 o'clock. Otherwise, put a check in the bottom left corner.

d. Draw a heart in the upper left corner if the squash match takes more than an hour. If it doesn't, put a check in the bottom left corner.

e. Draw a squiggly line connecting the last two figures you drew, not including check marks, if Mrs. Marshall doesn't have to pick up Sue after the match.

f. Draw a diamond at the top center of your paper if Mrs. Marshall's new dentist appointment is fifteen minutes earlier than her original appointment. If it isn't, put a check in the bottom left corner.

g. Draw a straight line from the triangle to a figure that does not have a line connecting it if Mr. and Mrs. Marshall have to have dinner before 7 o'clock. If they don't, put a check in the upper right corner.

h. Draw a circle in the center of your paper if Mrs. Marshall has planned four activities before her dentist appointment. If she hasn't, put a check in the bottom left corner.

i. Write your last name by the first figure you drew.

Reasoning

Introduction

To reason means:

1. to think;
2. to talk with another so as to influence his or her opinions or actions;
3. to discover or formulate by the use of reason; and
4. to exercise the faculty of logical thought.

In the first three units of this workbook you have been developing your ability to think clearly by learning to understand words and sentences and their relationships fully. In this unit the focus is on developing the specific skills one needs to carry out the three other definitions listed above, numbers 2 through 4. You will work on understanding how language is used to influence others' thinking. You will also work on the skills of problem solving and on certain forms of logical thought.

Before you begin, here are several basic points about reasoning and problem solving to think about.

1. Before you can solve a problem, you have to know what the problem is. The same is true if you are thinking about something in order to make a decision or draw a conclusion. Sometimes it is helpful to say to yourself, "Exactly what problem am I trying to solve?"

2. You may not always use all the information you've been given to solve a specific problem. It is important to learn to pick out the pieces of information you need to solve a problem. Here is an example:

> When Luciano visited the city, he always bought presents to take back to his family. He bought bagels for his sister and Chinese vegetables for his mother. His father usually asked for a special brand of pipe tobacco. His grandfather appreciated the Italian newspapers Luciano was able to buy in the city. He brought his wife herb teas and his children comic books.

Underline the information you need to figure out how many types of food Luciano brought back with him. Circle the information you need to figure out how many members of Luciano's family receive gifts when he returns from the city. The two problems require you to focus on different information.

3. Drawing a valid conclusion or reaching a satisfactory solution to a problem is not always easy. You have to think about whether or not you have enough firm evidence to draw your conclusion. Here is a simple example:

> Mr. Mink slammed the door.

Can we conclude that Mr. Mink is angry? Not necessarily. Perhaps a storm had blown the door open, and he had to slam it to get it shut again.

> Mr. Mink slammed the door after the boss told him he'd have to work on both Saturday and Sunday.

Now can we conclude that Mr. Mink is angry? We have reason to think he might be angry because he has to work all weekend. Our conclusion is a fairly sensible one, but there might be other explanations for his slamming the door.

In drawing conclusions, it is important to know when we can be certain whether one thing caused another. Do you see a causal relationship between the two events in this sentence?

Mrs. Winkler hung up the phone and then collapsed on her bed.

Would you say that the news she received on the phone caused her collapse? Are there other possible explanations?

4. We have to learn how to draw sound conclusions on the basis of generalizations. Here is a generalization.

All cars have wheels.

If we have a particular case, such as "A Ram is a car," can we conclude that a Ram has wheels? Yes, we can. But if we are told of something that has wheels, we cannot conclude that the object is a car. Other vehicles or objects have wheels. It might be a wheelchair or a wagon, for example.

With these points in mind, you are ready to start work on developing the skills we all use to think clearly and to solve problems.

Fact and Opinion

Two kinds of statements that we commonly hear and make ourselves are facts and opinions. Do you think you can tell the difference between the two kinds of statements? Try the sentences below. Label each fact **F** and each opinion **O**.

_____ 1. I believe that hamburgers are more popular than hot dogs.

_____ 2. Children are required by law to attend school.

_____ 3. Children under the age of six do not eat peas and spinach by choice.

_____ 4. I believe that sea water has a greater salt content than lake water.

As you thought about these statements, perhaps you noticed that sometimes a fact sounds like an opinion, and sometimes an opinion can sound like a fact. Statement #4 is a fact, but it is worded as if it were an opinion. Statement #3 is an opinion, but the forcefulness of the statement makes it sound like a fact.

What is the difference between the two kinds of statements? A **fact** is a statement of something that actually exists. To determine if a statement is factual, think about whether it can be proven to be true or shown to exist. In contrast, an **opinion** is a view, belief, or judgment. A person may believe it is true, but it cannot be proven or demonstrated as existing in reality. For example, it would be difficult, if not impossible, to prove that children under six don't eat peas by choice. On the other hand, it is possible to demonstrate that sea water has a greater salt content than lake water.

How could you show the following facts to be true? Think of a number of different ways.

1. Triangles have three sides. _____

_____

2. Poison ivy can cause a skin rash._____

_____

3. Chile is in southwestern South America. _____

_____

Fact and Opinion

In our daily life we all spend a fair amount of time sorting facts from opinions. It is important to learn to be critical and to think about information we hear or read before we accept it as fact. Opinions often pass as facts, and we can be led astray if we are too gullible—if we believe everything we read or hear. Certainly, advertisements make a business of convincing people that what is really just an opinion is a fact.

Here are some statements that may or may not truly be facts. Which ones seem acceptable to you? Check each one you think presents factual information. Be ready to discuss your reasoning.

_____ 1. Gentlemen prefer blondes.

_____ 2. Honey is better for you than sugar because it is a natural sweetener.

_____ 3. Children do better in school if they watch programs like "Sesame Street."

_____ 4. We conserve fuel resources and limit the pollution of the atmosphere when we use public transportation.

_____ 5. People who have life insurance worry less about the future.

_____ 6. You can prevent cavities by brushing your teeth at least twice a day, preferably after meals.

_____ 7. A trip to sunny Florida helps drive away winter blues.

_____ 8. A college education prepares tomorrow's world leaders.

_____ 9. Drinking milk helps children build strong bones and teeth.

_____ 10. A jeep can get you where you want to go.

Fact and Opinion

The purpose of this exercise is to see if you can tell a fact from an opinion. Label each fact **F** and each opinion **O**. Be ready to explain your answers.

_____ 1. Musicians are romantic.

_____ 2. You can make ice cream using a stove.

_____ 3. There are over 50,000 miles of railroad tracks in the United States.

_____ 4. Public universities have more competitive sports programs than private universities.

_____ 5. A tablespoon of peanut butter has more calories than half a cup of milk.

_____ 6. It is possible to send a telegram by telephone.

_____ 7. More women than men lose their car keys.

_____ 8. The wolf is related to the dog.

_____ 9. Forks with two prongs are easier to eat with than forks with three or four prongs.

_____ 10. Bees make wax.

_____ 11. One end of a slope must be higher than the other.

_____ 12. Every man is handsome when he wears a tuxedo.

_____ 13. The word *rhythm* is hard to spell correctly.

_____ 14. Only superstitious people believe in ghosts.

_____ 15. Clams can't survive outside of their shells.

_____ 16. A pair of scissors has two blades.

_____ 17. Anchovies ruin a good pizza.

_____ 18. A basket is a container made of woven material.

_____ 19. Mexicans hold more jobs in California than in North Dakota.

_____ 20. Scientists work for the benefit of humanity.

Judging Opinions

Most people express their opinions freely. Other people may or may not accept those opinions as reasonable, depending on their own beliefs. Here are several ways we can sort out opinions that are reasonable from those that are not.

1. We are more likely to consider an opinion reasonable if it is backed up by facts or supported by other reasonable statements. For example:

> Saul: "Dogs should not be fed sugar. It's bad for them."
> Paul: "Dogs should not be fed sugar. It causes their teeth to decay."

Whose opinion would you be more apt to consider reasonable? _____

2. We should consider *who* is stating the opinion before we place faith in it. If the speaker or writer is an expert or authority on the subject, we might accept the opinion more readily. If the person apparently has some sound knowledge or some experience, we might at least consider the opinion as a reasonable one. Here are examples. Whose opinion do you trust?

> "Renita told me that my hair would shine more if I washed it with raw eggs," said Betsy. (Who is Renita?)

> "Dr. Thompson suggested that I stop washing my hair every day for a while to keep it from getting so dry," said Kelly.

> "Use Shine on your hair daily for a quick way to that clean and alert feeling," said the radio announcer.

3. We are more willing to consider opinions if they sound reasonable.
We should be suspicious of opinions expressed with exaggeration; we
should also be careful to avoid appeals to accept ideas because everyone else does.
Finally, we should watch out for opinions that are meant to appeal to our emotions in order to win our support. Here are some examples:

> 1) Exaggeration: "Don't read any of the books on our reading list because they are all so boring that you'll be asleep in five minutes."

> 2) Bandwagon ("everyone else is"): "Don't sign up for the baseball team. No one I've heard about is at all interested in baseball this year."

> 3) An appeal to our emotions: "We must control the growth of industry if we are going to protect our nation's babies."

When you hear an opinion, you might consider accepting it if:
> a. it is supported by fact;
> b. it is stated by a person with authority, expertise, or experience; or,
> c. it is presented reasonably.

Judging Opinions

In the exercise below, you are asked to judge how reasonable a person's opinion seems to be. First, read each passage. Under each one, check whether or not you are willing to accept the speaker's opinion. If you accept the opinion, put down the number or numbers that show(s) your reason. Choose one of the following:

1. The speaker is an expert or has lots of experience in the area he or she is talking about.
2. The speaker supports his or her opinion with facts.

1. Bert says: "My uncle Allen says that schools don't teach kids to read any more. He ought to know what he is talking about. He's a proofreader for the *Morning Star.*"

   Accept opinion? No_____ Yes_____ Reason _____

2. Marvin says: "All I said was that the hospital guild was nothing but a collection of bored and frustrated people. Then Jody and another woman screamed all these arguments at me. Just goes to show you, Harry, you can't say anything critical to women. They're too emotional."

   Accept opinion? No_____ Yes_____ Reason _____

3. Alison Black: "It really is a shame that the Department of Health has prevented the sale of that drug. Research on animals has shown that the drug has no harmful side effects, and it has been used legally in England for three years. The doctors there think it is very successful in controlling high blood pressure."

   Accept opinion? No_____ Yes_____ Reason _____

4. Pete says: "You've got to try Mario's pizza. It's the best in town. We took our kids there the other night. We ate two large pizzas down to the last crust. They really put good stuff on top."

   Accept opinion? No_____ Yes_____ Reason _____

5. Mrs. Wickers says: "I've been running this hospital for three years, and I'll tell you, the nurses are really underpaid. The nurses at Highview get about $1000 more a week. Our nurses often do work that is as specialized as that the doctors do."

   Accept opinion? No_____ Yes_____ Reason _____

6. Mr. Sorensen (teacher): "Nuclear war will destroy the civilization we know on earth. If you don't believe me, just wait."

   Accept opinion? No_____ Yes_____ Reason _____

Relevant Information

Faced with a problem to solve or a decision that has to be made, you need to be able to figure out whether or not you can solve the problem with the information you are given. You also need to figure out which pieces of information you are going to need to use. The bits of information that you use to help yourself solve particular problems or answer specific questions are called **relevant information**.

Yvette put her glasses, keys, and handkerchief into her handbag and headed for the gas station. On the way, she stopped at the drug store to buy tissues and a package of gum. When she reached the service station she couldn't find her wallet in her handbag, but she did find her checkbook, so she was able to pay for the new muffler and exhaust pipe. Then she drove home.

How many items do we know Yvette carries in her handbag? _____ Circle each bit of information that will help you answer this question.

How many stops does Yvette make? _____ Underline the bits of information that are relevant to this question.

Now read the paragraph that follows. You'll be asked two questions at the end of it. Then you will be asked to find the pieces of information that were relevant to each of the questions.

In five years of hard work, Karen had held three different jobs and had earned $50,000. She had paid off her educational loan ($3,000) and the car she had bought when she graduated from college ($4,000). This year she decided she was going to look seriously for a higher paying job.

Question 1: About how much money did Karen earn each year? _____

_____ Circle the pieces of information that you used to answer this question.

Question 2: What major debts did Karen pay off? _____

_____ Underline the pieces of information you found that helped you answer this question.

From this exercise you should see that information that is relevant in answering one question is not necessarily relevant in answering other questions.

Relevant Information

This is an exercise to see if you can find relevant information.

Mr. and Mrs. Jones and their children live in Brooklyn, New York. The children are Sam, Barbara, and Dennis. The family is discussing a camping trip they are planning to take this summer. They are trying to decide **where** and **when** to take their trip.

The following is a list of points that come up in their discussion. Check the points that are relevant to the decisions they are trying to make.

_____ 1. Mr. Jones is looking for someone to water the plants while they are away.

_____ 2. Dennis is a Cub Scout.

_____ 3. Sam has signed up for a series of four lessons in gymnastics in July.

_____ 4. Dennis got car sick on last year's trip, but Mrs. Jones thinks he had the flu.

_____ 5. Sam collects rocks and loves to go mountain climbing.

_____ 6. Mr. Jones found a four-person tent on sale in a catalog.

_____ 7. No one except Barbara wants to go back to the Everglades, where they went last year.

_____ 8. Mrs. Jones has appointments to see two very important new clients in the first week of August.

_____ 9. Barbara wants to invite Michele Andrews, her best friend.

_____ 10. Mr. Jones is eager to have the children meet their Great Aunt Elizabeth, who has just moved from California to Maine.

Relevant Information

Read the paragraphs. Then answer the question.

At the start of the baseball season there were eighteen boys on the Hawks, Somerville's town team. During the summer, five of the boys dropped off the team. The Hawks played sixteen games that season. Just for fun they also played two games against Little League teams and one game against their fathers. The Hawks won half the games they played against other town teams. They tied one and won one against the Little League teams. However, they lost to their fathers.

Last year they played four more regular season games than they did this year. They won half their games, tied two, and lost the rest. They played against the Little League teams three times, winning each game. However, they lost to their fathers.

Question: How many regular season games did the Hawks win last year? _____

Now, check each statement that gives information relevant to solving the problem.

_____ 1. There were eighteen boys on the Hawks at first.

_____ 2. Five boys dropped off the team.

_____ 3. The Hawks played sixteen season games this year.

_____ 4. They played two games against Little League teams and one against their fathers.

_____ 5. The Hawks won half their regular games this year.

_____ 6. The Hawks won one of their Little League games this year.

_____ 7. Last year the Hawks played four more regular games than they did this year.

_____ 8. The Hawks won half their regular season games last year.

_____ 9. They tied two regular season games last year and lost the rest.

_____ 10. The team lost to their fathers both years.

Relevant Information

When you have to make a decision there is usually one main issue — sometimes even two or three — that must be taken into account in order to make a wise decision. Sometimes you can sort out poor arguments from good arguments by figuring out which ones truly focus on the basic issue or issues. The arguments that do focus on the main issue can be considered relevant.

For example, if Helena is going sailing tomorrow, but her father is unsure whether or not it is safe for her to sail alone, checking the weather could prove to be quite relevant to the decision. If the day were to be stormy, sailing alone would not be safe. The father's request that Helena wash the family car would not be relevant.

Here is the problem that requires a decision:

Mr. and Mrs. Blackburn bought a Tanto station wagon two years ago. They have had a series of problems with the car ever since they got it, and the expenses have added up. Now the car needs to have its transmission repaired, which will be very expensive. They are trying to decide whether to repair the car or to sell it and buy a new car. Mr. Blackburn wants to get rid of the Tanto and get a new car.

Here are the arguments Mr. Blackburn is using to convince his wife that they should get a new car. Check (✔) each statement that is relevant to the problem. Remember that the issue as we know it is the expense of keeping the Tanto running well. Be ready to discuss your reasons for checking or not checking each statement.

_____ 1. We don't need such a large car.

_____ 2. We just finished paying for the last repair they did on the Tanto.

_____ 3. Susie's infant seat doesn't fit in well.

_____ 4. Buying gas is getting to be more and more expensive.

_____ 5. In the long run, a new car will cost less than keeping up the old Tanto.

_____ 6. Mr. Jones said he'd give us a $1,000 trade-in on a new car, and that's pretty good.

_____ 7. The Tanto has always been hard to fit in the garage.

_____ 8. This car has so many engine problems already that it's bound to have more.

_____ 9. There is a nice-looking blue Intrepid in the showroom at Reynolds Motors.

_____ 10. What are we going to do if the car breaks down in the middle of our trip this summer?

Relevant Information

Here is another problem in which you'll be figuring out the issues and the information relevant to solving the problem.

Colleen is a trained typist. She was graduated from vocational school this spring. She needs to get a job to support her mother and herself. She has been looking for a job as a typist, but the only job offer she has gotten is a position as a filing clerk for a large company. She is talking to her friend Mary about whether or not she should take the job offer.

What are the *two* issues that you can see are important in making this decision? _____

_____

Using these two issues to guide you, check each of Colleen's statements that are relevant in making this important decision.

_____ 1. The office I'd spend most of my time in is ugly.

_____ 2. I don't know how to run a big filing system.

_____ 3. It's such a large company that maybe I'll get a job typing for them soon.

_____ 4. Betsy's brother works in their shipping and receiving department, and Betsy says he hates it.

_____ 5. I should accept this job, and then try to get some typing work to do in the evenings so that I can keep my typing speed up.

_____ 6. I really want a job nearer our apartment so that I can run home at lunchtime.

_____ 7. The manager says they give super pay raises if you do a good job.

_____ 8. I applied for seven other jobs and didn't get any other offer.

_____ 9. My sister says I'm too talented for a job like this.

_____ 10. I'm never going to meet any new people if I have my head in a filing cabinet all day.

Inference

An **inference** is a judgment or conclusion that explains one or more observations. We all make inferences as we try to organize and understand all that we observe, hear, and read. The inference that Judy makes below is the kind we make as we go about our daily lives.

> Judy saw that the clock in the front hall said ten o'clock as she came in. While she was closing the front door, her father said sternly, "Judith, come here right now!" Judy inferred that he was angry that she was late.

Since inferences are our way of understanding what goes on around us, learning to make valid inferences is very important indeed. It is not always easy. Sometimes the observations or clues that you have to go on are not adequate. Sometimes we can make a number of possible inferences, so that no single explanation is more likely to be true. Here are examples of these two types of problems.

> Eight-year-old Richie ran across the yard and into the kitchen, crying. "Mom!" he yelled. "Dad!"

We don't have enough information in this situation to make a sensible inference. Richie could be either injured or scared. Perhaps a friend insulted him or took his tricycle away.

> When Mr. Sawyer got to his car in the far corner of the city parking lot, he saw that his front left tire was flat. Looking around, he noticed two cars nearby that also had flat tires.

We have quite a few clues in this situation, but they do not form a clear pattern. Several explanations are possible. Can you think of two? However, no one explanation seems more likely to be true than the others.

We must learn to evaluate inferences in order to figure out how much faith we can put in them. First, we need to think about whether or not an inference is *reasonable*. Does it take into account all of the clues, and is it a sensible explanation? This is *not* a sensible inference:

> The apples on the table are green. Inference: They must be rotten.

Second, we need to figure out whether or not a given explanation is a likely explanation or only one of a number of possible explanations. With these points in mind, try evaluating the following inferences. First, is the inference a reasonable one? If it is reasonable, can you think of other possible explanations, or is this the most likely explanation? Discuss these two problems.

1. The electricity went out at 10 P.M. in the Grossman's house. Natalie inferred that a storm was coming.

2. At seven o'clock on Sunday night Harold walked past Stalner's Seafood Restaurant and noticed that very few people were eating there. He inferred that their food must not be very appealing.

Inference

The purpose of this exercise is to see if you can distinguish information that is stated directly from inferences. First read the passage. Then follow the directions given below.

On Friday night David and Kathy decided to go to a popular movie called *The Shadow*. They went to the early show because Kathy's parents wanted her home by 10 o'clock. When they got to the theater on Oak Street at 6:30, they found that a line of people waiting to buy tickets extended down the block and around the corner. Instead of standing in line, David and Kathy went to get a soda at the drugstore across the street. They returned in twenty minutes. The line was still at least a block long. They waited in line for twenty minutes. By then they were halfway up the line, and they figured that there were about thirty people ahead of them. They knew the movie would have started by then, so they gave up and went home. They watched a movie called *The Long Day* on TV at Kathy's house.

Write **D** before each statement that gives information directly stated in the passage. Before each inference write **I**.

_____ 1. The movie began at 7 o'clock.

_____ 2. *The Shadow* was a popular movie.

_____ 3. Kathy had to be home by 10 o'clock.

_____ 4. There would be a long line of people for the late show that night.

_____ 5. They arrived at the Oak Street theater at 6:30.

_____ 6. David and Kathy wanted to see the whole movie from beginning to end.

_____ 7. *The Shadow* was showing at the theater on Oak Street.

_____ 8. David and Kathy like soda.

_____ 9. David and Kathy don't like waiting in line.

_____ 10. Kathy's parents are strict.

_____ 11. About the time the movie started there were about thirty people in line ahead of them.

_____ 12. Across the street from the movie theatre is a drugstore.

Inference

It is not always possible to make an inference that is a reliable explanation of what has been observed. One reason is that the bits of information we call clues do not present a clear enough pattern. In this exercise you must decide if you have enough clues to make a reasonable inference. If you do, write the inference on the lines. If you don't, write MIN (for "more information needed") on the line.

1. The woman was walking very rapidly down the street. She was carrying a white paper bag in her right hand. The bag had printing on it that read: "Ike's Ice Cream — The Best in Town." It sure was a hot day for her to be rushing along so quickly.

   Clues: walking rapidly   Inference: _____
          white paper bag
          "Ike's Ice   _____
          Cream"
          hot day   _____

2. When Dr. Harris went to feed the fish in the aquarium, she realized that the two angel fish were not in the tank. The other fish seemed to be swimming around normally. The water filter was running, and the water was clear.

   Clues: feeding fish   Inference_____
          fish missing
          filter running   _____
          water clear
          other fish   _____
            normal

3. When I got home at 5:30, our car was gone. Aunt Caroline's car was parked in the driveway. Pa is usually home from work before 5:30, but neither Ma nor Pa was home. As a matter of fact, the dogs were gone too. Even the dogs' leashes were gone.

   Clues: our car gone   Inference: _____
          Caroline's car
          no one home   _____
          leashes gone
                              _____

4. Mr. Samuels was reading in his living room. Suddenly his front window exploded, scattering glass all over the room. A baseball banged against the living room wall. Mr. Samuels sat in shock for a moment. Then he leaped out of his chair and ran to the window. Across the street he saw Hank and Paula Smith, his neighbor's children, staring in his direction.

   Clues: broken window   Inference: _____
          baseball
          children staring   _____

                              _____

Inference

Read each situation below. Study the clues and the inference that is made to explain the situation. If you think the inference is the most likely explanation of what happened, write YES on the line. If you think it is only one of a number of possible explanations, write POSSIBLE on the line. Then list two other possible explanations on the lines below.

1. Mrs. Selino was just coming out of her house to go to work when she noticed a truck coming down Oak Street. The truck was moving very slowly, but it was weaving back and forth across the road. There was no other traffic in its way. Mrs. Selino wondered if the driver had fallen asleep.

Inference _____

Other possible explanations:

1._____

2._____

2. When Phyllis got on the elevator at the first floor, she was the only person in the elevator. She pushed the button for the seventh floor, because she was on her way to the insurance company office. The elevator started up. She watched the light as it showed each floor she went by. She saw that the elevator was stopping at the fifth floor. Phyllis wondered if the elevator had broken down.

Inference _____

Other possible explanations:

1._____

2._____

3. Mr. Maxwell turned on the water faucet in the kitchen. Only a dribble of water came out. Then he tried the faucet in the bathroom. Same problem. When he opened the cellar door to check the water pressure, he heard water pouring onto the cellar floor. He figured the main water pipe had burst.

Inference _____

Other possible explanations:

1._____

2._____

Inference

In this exercise you will be evaluating inferences made on the basis of information given in the passage. Check each statement that seems to be a good inference. Write DN on the line if we don't know enough to make the inference, and write O if the inference is simply not a reasonable one.

John figured that he had to earn $500 during the summer in order to buy a motorcycle. He tried hard to get a job painting so he could be outside during the day. He had also heard from a friend that you earn a lot painting houses. He was offered a job as a dishwasher in a restaurant for the dinner shift, but he turned that down. Instead he took a job as a lifeguard. He earned $450. He knew his father would lend him the remaining $50 if he paid it back in a month or two. All in all, he felt that his summer had been worthwhile.

_____ 1. John has a motorcycle already.

_____ 2. The motorcycle John wanted to buy cost $500.

_____ 3. John has saved other money that he can use to help pay for the motorcycle.

_____ 4. John likes to work outside.

_____ 5. John likes to paint.

_____ 6. John could not find a painting job.

_____ 7. John disliked his job as a lifeguard.

_____ 8. John was able to work outdoors at his job.

_____ 9. John will soon be able to get the motorcycle he wanted.

_____ 10. John's father has refused to lend him money.

_____ 11. John was pleased with his summer.

_____ 12. John would earn more money painting houses than washing dishes.

_____ 13. John was a good lifeguard.

_____ 14. John's father diaspproved of John's plan to buy a motorcycle.

Inference

First read the general statement, then read each particular situation presented below, checking each inference as reasonable or not. Be ready to discuss your reasoning.

Several reliable surveys have shown that people who have spent an average of fifty hours or more a week at a single job for more than six months become exhausted and depressed.

1. Angela has worked as a supervisor for Speedways Corporation for fifteen years. Can we reasonably infer that she is exhausted and depressed?

    Yes _____ No _____

2. Mac works the eight-hour night shift at Peerless Plastics. Some afternoons he works for the YMCA as a janitor. He catches up on his sleep over the weekends. Can we reasonably infer that Mac is exhausted and depressed?

    Yes _____ No _____

3. For the past two years Ellen has been supporting her family as well as paying a nurse to care for her ailing father. She has a 9 to 5 job as a salesclerk at Iggie's and works at least three hours overtime every day. Can we reasonably infer that Ellen is exhausted and depressed?

    Yes _____ No _____

4. John spent the summer in Alaska. He had trouble finding a summer job, but he finally got a job in a canning factory at the height of the salmon season. He worked ten hours a day, with Sundays off. Can we reasonably infer that John is exhausted and depressed?

    Yes _____ No _____

5. Fifty-year-old Jerry Thompson has been a coal miner all his adult life. The whistle calling the miners to work blows at sunrise. He is home most days for dinner at 5 o'clock. Can we reasonably infer that Jerry is exhausted and depressed?

    Yes _____ No _____

6. Frank Pressman got a job as a clerk at Southeast Electric when he graduated from college last year. He works a regular nine-to-five shift, although he has come in to work on a number of Saturdays when the boss has needed his help. Frank has been having serious headaches. Can we reasonably infer he is depressed?

    Yes _____ No _____

Cause-Effect

When one thing makes another happen, we label the relationship between the two events **cause-effect**. Some cause-effect relationships are quite easy to recognize. For example, Hannah dropped a plate and it broke. We can safely say that dropping the plate caused it to break. However, not all cause-effect patterns are so simple to see.

People are likely to make one of four different kinds of errors in labeling the relationship between two events cause-effect. These problems in recognizing cause-effect relationships are discussed below.

Problem 1: We have to be careful about assigning causation when we are not really sure of the cause. Here is an example:

> Uncle Ted argued with Martha yesterday. Martha didn't show up to mow his lawn for him today.

We can't be certain that the argument caused Martha to stay away from Uncle Ted or her job. Perhaps she was sick. Perhaps an emergency came up. We should not say that one event caused another unless we are sure that there are no other possible explanations.

Problem 2: Just because two events happen one after the other does not mean that the first event caused the second. For example:

> After Mrs. Signolio left the office, her secretary started typing.

We cannot say that Mrs. Signolio's leaving the office caused the secretary to start typing. As far as we can see, these events are simply related by **time order** — one comes after the other.

Problem 3: Direct causation and indirect causation are different, and we should be careful to distinguish the two. Causation is direct when one event clearly triggers the next. Hannah's breaking of the plate is an example. Here is another example:

> Kerry tripped on the rope and fell.

Indirect causation occurs with a series or chain of cause-effect relationships. The two events are indirectly related if they do *not* happen right after each other. Here is an example:

> Because Mr. Hafner's brakes failed, Mr. Cohen drove his car into our stone wall.

The failure of Mr. Hafner's brakes indirectly caused Mr. Cohen's accident. Mr. Hafner was unable to stop at the Stop sign. Luckily, Mr. Cohen saw him racing toward the crossroads, so he veered to the right. Because he was unable to steer his car back onto the road, he ran into the stone wall.

Here is another illustration of indirect causation.

> Since Nancy went to the doctor, her rash went away.

We cannot say that the doctor directly caused Nancy's skin to heal. The doctor gave Nancy the proper medicine to put on the rash. It is the medicine that caused the rash to go away. We could say that the doctor *indirectly* caused Nancy's skin to heal.

Problem 4: One event can have several causes or several results. In a situation like this, it is incorrect to list just one of the causes or effects. Here is an example:

John stayed up late, and the next day he failed a history test.
He was too exhausted to be able to pass the test.

In fact, there is an additional cause that is not mentioned here. John had not kept up with his studying. That is why he was working so late at night. It would be more accurate to say that he failed the test because he was behind in his studies and because he was exhausted.

All four of these possible errors in cause-effect reasoning should be kept in mind when you are considering drawing the conclusion that two events are related by causation.

Cause-Effect

Not one of the examples below has a simple, direct cause-effect relationship. Each of them fits one (or possibly two) of the categories listed below:

    A. The example gives a **time-order** relationship
       (one thing happens after another).
    B. The example is part of a **chain of causation** (indirect causation).
    C. **Not enough information** is given to be certain of the cause.

Read each example. Then label it **A**, **B**, or **C** to show the type of relationship in that example. You may put down two letters if you think two explanations are possible. Be ready to explain your choice.

_____ 1. One cold night the Smiths stoked their wood-burning stove well before they went to bed. Their house burned down in the middle of the night.

_____ 2. Marilyn jogged for five miles. Then, after her shower, she ate a big breakfast.

_____ 3. At ten o'clock last night Grandfather went outside without his cane. He slipped on a patch of ice by the back door and broke his hip badly.

_____ 4. Bobby borrowed my math book yesterday to study for the quiz. As for me, I failed the quiz.

_____ 5. It has been raining all day. Everything was damp — our clothes, the ground, the wood, the matches, our food, even the air. Mr. Bartol couldn't get the campfire lit.

_____ 6. The Travises asked Gary to water their houseplants while they were away on vacation. Ten of the plants were dead when they got back.

_____ 7. Katharine finished all her homework before she went to the movie with Edith.

_____ 8. Jane came down with the flu. She ended up staying home for two weeks. She had to try to to do her homework on her own. Her grades dropped during that marking period.

_____ 9. Our dog Fluffy was barking furiously, but we couldn't find anyone at the door or around the house.

_____ 10. While the two men were splitting the logs the children stacked the split wood in the garage.

Cause-Effect

Read each problem below. Then answer the questions.

1. Mrs. Black was getting twenty miles to the gallon driving her car on highways for the last three months—September–November. She just had the car serviced and the engine carefully tuned. For the last week she has been getting twenty-eight miles to the gallon driving on the same highways at the same speed. She figures the servicing and tuning of her car has improved the mileage she is getting for each gallon of gas.

   1. What cause-effect relationship does Mrs. Black see here? _____

      _____

      _____

   2. Is this good cause-effect reasoning? Explain. _____

      _____

      _____

      _____

2. Stephen is a better car salesperson than any of the other men and women at Reynolds Motors. He is a friendly man. He also is an excellent golfer and a member of the town council. But he knows the people who work with him don't like him very much. He thinks that they are jealous of him. He feels that if they can't accept the fact that some people are more successful than others, that's their tough luck. So he stays away from them and just works at selling cars.

   1. What cause-effect relationship does Stephen see? _____

      _____

      _____

   2. Does this description suggest another cause for Stephen's unpopularity? Explain.

      _____

      _____

      _____

      _____

      _____

Cause-Effect

Read each problem below. Then answer the questions.

1. Grandfather refuses to go to the hospital, even though his doctor has told him that he should. His reasoning is as follows: The hospital is full of sick people. Sickness is caused by germs. Germs spread, no matter what people do to try to prevent their spreading. Germs cause diseases. He already has one disease. He knows that when you are sick, your body is not as able to fight germs and diseases. So he figures that there is a very good chance he'd get sicker at the hospital instead of getting over the illness he already has. He thinks that the hospital is the last thing he needs. He is an old man, and he wants to live his old age in good health.

   Which parts of grandfather's reasoning show good cause-effect reasoning? List them below.

   _____

   _____

   _____

   List below any parts of grandfather's reasoning that don't seem to you to show good reasoning.

   _____

   _____

   _____

2. Many people feel that the best way to prevent wars is to make an agreement between nations *not* to build up their armed forces or develop and stock up weapons used in war.

   This reasoning involves a cause-effect relationship that is not stated here. What is this cause-effect relationship? Complete the statement.

   _____ causes _____.

   Do weapons cause war or do people cause war? Can you choose one or the other?

   _____

   Explain your reasoning: _____

   _____

   _____

Syllogisms

A syllogism is a logical analysis of a formal argument. This definition may sound strange and new to you, but the syllogism starts out with the kind of statement you have studied already — the generalization. For example:

Every house has walls.

In the presentation of a syllogism, the generalization is followed by a specific case, such as, "The pueblo is a kind of house." Then a conclusion is drawn using the generalization and the specific case. In this case, we could conclude that a pueblo has walls. Here is a second example:

All carpenters use hammers.
Josie is a carpenter.
Conclusion: Josie uses a hammer.

The next step in working with a syllogism is your analysis of the reasoning. Since Josie is a carpenter, she falls into the category of "all carpenters." And since *all* carpenters use hammers, Josie must use a hammer. The reasoning is valid.

By way of comparison, here are two examples in which the reasoning of the syllogism is not valid.

Some pilots wear uniforms.
Sandy is a pilot.
Conclusion: Sandy wears a uniform.

Notice that the generalization in this syllogism says *some* pilots. Sandy could either be one of the pilots that does wear a uniform or one of the pilots that does not wear a uniform. Therefore, we cannot conclude that Sandy wears a uniform.

All monkeys eat bananas.
Amanda eats bananas.
Conclusion: Amanda is a monkey.

This time the second statement does *not* tell us that Amanda is a monkey. It tells us that Amanda shares the characteristic of eating bananas. However, monkeys are not the only creatures that eat bananas. Therefore, even though Amanda eats bananas, we cannot conclude that she is a monkey. As a result, this syllogism also has what we call an invalid conclusion.

Read the following syllogism. Is the conclusion valid or invalid? _____

Most hamsters eat lettuce.
Bertha is my sister's pet hamster.
Conclusion: Bertha must eat lettuce.

Syllogisms

Each of the syllogisms in this exercise fits one of the three patterns you have just worked on. Write **valid** on the line if the conclusion is a good one. Write **invalid** on the line if the conclusion is based on poor reasoning. Be ready to explain your answers.

1. All monkeys climb trees.
   Bumpy is a monkey.
   Conclusion: Bumpy climbs trees.   _____

2. All monkeys climb trees.
   Pat climbs trees.
   Conclusion: Pat is a monkey.   _____

3. Some monkeys eat bananas.
   Sandy is a monkey.
   Conclusion: Sandy eats bananas.   _____

4. All trees have leaves.
   A mosk is a tree.
   Conclusion: A mosk has leaves.   _____

5. All fish can swim.
   Ginger can swim.
   Conclusion: Ginger is a fish.   _____

6. Some men have beards.
   Peter is a man.
   Conclusion: Peter has a beard.   _____

7. All thumpers have pink noses.
   Zing is a thumper.
   Conclusion: Zing has a pink nose.   _____

8. Most knives have sharp blades.
   This is a knife.
   Conclusion: It has a sharp blade.   _____

9. All carpenters work with hammers.
   Ms. Dow is working with a hammer.
   Conclusion: Ms. Dow is a carpenter.   _____

10. Most klims are sluvvy and eb.
    Dribble is a klim.
    Conclusion: Dribble is sluvvy and eb.   _____

Syllogisms

Another type of syllogism uses a negative in the general statement.

>No worms have legs.
>Squirm is a worm.
>Conclusion: Squirm does not have legs.

The general statement tells you that *not one* member of the group (worms) fits the statement. If Squirm is a member of the group called worms, Squirm cannot have legs.

>Elephants never live two hundred years.
>Star is an elephant.
>Conclusion: Star can never live two hundred years.

In the problems below, there are examples of all four types of syllogisms. Figure out if the conclusion shows good reasoning. If the conclusion is a good one, write **valid** on the line. If the conclusion does not show good reasoning, write **invalid** on the line.

1. Some soldiers fight in wars.
   Joe is a soldier.
   Conclusion: He fights in wars.   _____

2. All cars have wheels.
   The Wildcat is a car.
   Conclusion: It has wheels.   _____

3. Anteaters are never kept as house pets.
   Tiny is an anteater.
   Conclusion: Tiny is not kept as a house pet.   _____

4. All birds lay eggs.
   The thab lays eggs.
   Conclusion: The thab is a bird.   _____

5. Most bottles hold liquids.
   That green container is a bottle.
   Conclusion: That green container might hold a liquid,
      and it might not.   _____

6. No rose bush has blue flowers.
   This bush is a rose bush.
   Conclusion: It can't have blue flowers.   _____

7. All rangles have wups.
   Bumpy has a wup.
   Conclusion: Bumpy is a rangle.   _____

8. Zinks never swamp stangles.
   Rep is a zink.
   Conclusion: Rep will swamp a stangle.   _____

Syllogisms

All the problems below are syllogisms. Figure out what conclusion can be made after you have read the first two statements. Write your conclusion on the line.

1. Magazines always have advertisements.
   Today is a magazine.

   Conclusion: _____

   _____

2. Some tables are used for eating.
   That piece of furniture is a table.

   Conclusion: _____

   _____

3. All giraffes have long necks.
   Crump has a long neck.

   Conclusion: _____

   _____

4. No fish has feathers.
   A bisk is a fish.

   Conclusion: _____

   _____

5. All human beings make mistakes.
   Science teachers are human beings.

   Conclusion: _____

   _____

6. Most movie stars are charming.
   John Jeffrey is a movie star.

   Conclusion: _____

   _____

7. Rugs are never used to cover ceilings.
   That piece of material is a rug.

   Conclusion: _____

   _____

Problems and Practice

Solving word problems requires that you use many of the different skills you have been working on. You need to be able to work out the meanings of individual sentences and to see how the different pieces of information in a problem are related to each other. You need to be able to figure out which pieces of information are relevant to solving the problem or answering different questions. Often you need to make reasonable inferences and draw sound conclusions.

Over the next few pages you will have a number of different kinds of word problems to solve. Do your best to apply the skills you have been working on as you tackle each problem.

On the last day of the fair the man who sold popcorn made $500. He put $300 in the bank and spent the rest on new clothes and a plane ticket to New York. His new suit cost him $75. His plane flies at midnight.

Label each statement **T** for true, **F** for false, or **CT** for can't tell.

_____ 1. The fair was in town for more than one day.

_____ 2. The man spent $150 on clothes.

_____ 3. The trip cost $125.

_____ 4. The man had sold popcorn at other fairs.

_____ 5. The man is going to fly to New York.

_____ 6. The man saved less than half his day's earnings.

_____ 7. The man bought the new suit for himself.

_____ 8. Other food besides popcorn was sold at the fair.

_____ 9. The man usually didn't make $500 in one day.

_____ 10. The man who sold popcorn also bought a plane ticket to New York.

Problems and Practice

Read the problem. Then do the exercise that follows it.

1. Five children rowed in four boats across a river. Three of them rowed back in two of the boats to pick up four more friends.

    1. How many children crossed the river? _____

    2. How many times did the boats go back and forth across the river? _____

    3. How many boats did the children use? _____

    4. Did the two groups cross the same river? Yes_____ No_____

    How can you tell? _____

2. At 8 o'clock yesterday morning Betsy left Easton to go to Wilton. She started so early that she was rather sleepy, so before reaching Sommerville she stopped for a cup of coffee. Although she drove through Greenville, she stopped at Oakville for lunch. As she started to pay for her lunch, she discovered that she had left her wallet in Sommerville at a gas station. Luckily, she knew the owner of the diner, so she was able to leave without paying. She drove back to Sommerville, where she picked up her wallet and returned to pay for her lunch.

Since it was midafternoon, she hurried through Westport, although she should have stopped to see her cousin. She thought she might have dinner in Bedford at a restaurant she had heard was quite good unless some close friends of hers in South Bedford were home. When she called from Bedford, her friends asked her to dinner, so she went to their house. Before going on to Wilton for the night, she told her friends about her busy day and the many stops she had had to make.

How many stops had she made? _____

3. The football team from Westfield won five games during the season. They lost four games and tied two. They played eleven games during the season. Last year the team played ten games during the season, winning six of them.

Label each of the following statements **T** (true), **F** (false) or **CT** (can't tell whether the statement is true or false).

_____ 1. This year the football team won more games than it lost.

_____ 2. The football team is made up only of boys who live in Westfield.

_____ 3. Sometimes the football team neither wins nor loses a game.

_____ 4. The football team played nine games altogether this year.

_____ 5. Both years the football team has had a winning season (more wins than losses).

_____ 6. Last year the team did not win more games than it lost during the season.

_____ 7. The same group of boys has played football for Westfield for two years.

_____ 8. This year the team played two games before or after the season.

_____ 9. This year the team lost more games than last year.

_____ 10. Last year the team did not tie any of its season games.

4. A triangle sits in the middle of a row of six squares. Some of the squares are taller than the triangle, and some are not. Draw a picture that shows which squares are taller than the triangle and which are not, using the following clues:

    1. Two to the left are taller; two to the right are smaller than the triangle.
    2. No tall square sits next to another tall square.

Draw the row of figures here:

Problems and Practice — Using Charts and Diagrams

Many word problems are easier to solve if you can draw a picture or chart to portray the information given in the problem. If you can see the relationships between the pieces of information in the problem, you can usually reason the solution more clearly.

Look at the problem below. Then look at the diagram that shows you the relationships in size.

Grandfather says that the radio tower is taller than the church steeple, but that the observation tower at the airport is not as high as the church steeple. Which of the three structures is the tallest?

radio tower   church   observation tower

A chart is another way to rank the structures in height. Here is an example of this method of solving the problem.

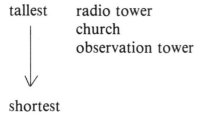

tallest   radio tower
church
observation tower

shortest

The problems below are similar to this problem. Each asks you to compare at least three things. Draw a chart or diagram to solve each one. Use extra paper. Some of the problems ask a question that cannot be answered with the information given. Be careful!

1. In the spring, dandelions bloom before roses, and daffodils bloom before dandelions. Which flower blooms first? Which flower blooms last?

2. Bessie has more books than Tessie. Tillie has fewer books than Bessie. Which girl has the most books?

3. If Frank's dog is smaller and older than Tom's, and Don's dog is smaller but younger than Tom's, which dog is the smallest? Which one is the oldest?

4. Peanuts cost more than almonds. Pecans cost more than walnuts and more than peanuts. Walnuts cost less than almonds. Which of the nuts costs most? Which one costs least?

5. Hilda, Happy, and Hester are three kittens from the same litter. The darkest kitten is also the smallest one. Happy is darker than Hester but not darker than Hilda. Which kitten is the darkest? Which is the lightest? Which kitten is the smallest? Which one is the largest?

6. Elaine runs faster than Sam, but Sam runs faster than Elaine's cousin, Jacob. Does Jacob run faster or slower than Elaine?

7. Maple sugar has more calories per tablespoon than cream, which has more calories than applesauce. Martha's dessert of applesauce, cream, and maple sugar still has fewer calories than the custard Dan makes. List the foods in order of numbers of calories, most to least.

Problems and Practice — Deductive Reasoning

In solving problems that use deductive reasoning, figure out what you *don't* know by eliminating all possibilities based on what you *do* know. Here is an example:

One of the three Pine children ate all of the brownies that Chester baked. Susie was babysitting for Ted and Leslie while their parents were out. Ted is one year old. He took a nap and played in his playpen. Leslie hates sweets and is allergic to chocolate. Which of the children ate the brownies ?

Because we can see that Ted and Leslie did not eat the brownies, we can be certain that Susie ate the brownies.

Often the easiest way to work out a problem of this type is to make a chart.

Read the problem below and then study the chart that follows it.

Jill, Will, and Tim work at the zoo in Washington, each one in charge of a particular area: the large cats, the reptiles, or the bird house. Jill is frightened of reptiles. During their lunch break, Jill and Will bring their sandwiches to the bird house to have lunch with Tim, since he seldom has more than a few minutes off. Which person is in charge of which area of the zoo?

	Cats	Reptiles	Birds
Jill		✕	✕
Will		✔	✕
Tim			✔

The chart has been filled in with the information given in the problem. **X** stands for a combination that we know is *not* true. For example, the **X** at the spot where Jill and reptiles meet shows that Jill does *not* take care of the reptiles. An ✔ stands for a combination that is true.

See if you can fill out the rest of the chart. For example, if Tim is in charge of the bird house, he cannot be in charge of the reptiles or the large cats. Put an **X** by Tim's name under the Cats and Reptiles columns. Can you see who must be caring for the reptiles and the cats?

Problems and Practice

Make a chart to solve each of the problems below.

1. Dingle, Spangle, and Simple are puppies from the same litter of terriers. Each has a different appearance. Dingle doesn't have a black tail or brown patches over his eyes. Simple is the smallest. The largest of the puppies has a black tail. One of the three puppies is all white. Figure out what each of the puppies looks like.

2. Dan, Meg, and Fred were playing baseball one morning. Then they played all over the neighborhood. Next they realized that they had all left their baseball mitts somewhere. They couldn't remember where they had put them down. Each person had left a mitt in a different place. "I didn't put mine in the tree house," said Meg. "I'm sure I didn't leave mine at the baseball field," said Dan. "I didn't either," said Fred. "And I know I had my mitt with me after we went swimming."

   Which person left a mitt in the tree house? _____

   Which person left a mitt at the baseball field? _____

   Which person put a mitt down by the pond? _____

Problems and Practice

Make a chart to solve this first problem.

1. Last Saturday Mr. Smith, Mr. Brown, and Mrs. Jones each bought a car from the same used-car dealer. The three cars they bought were a station wagon, a jeep, and a sedan. Mr. Smith couldn't afford the sedan. Mr. Brown did not want the station wagon because it was too big. Mrs. Jones felt the same way, but she liked the car that Mr. Smith decided against. Which car did each of the three end up buying?

Make two columns (one for height, the other for age) to solve this problem.

2. John, Joan, Jane, and Jeff are the names of four Johnson children. Their ages and heights are all different. Use the information in the following sentences to figure out the order of the children by age (starting with the oldest) and their order in height (starting with the tallest).

   a. Jane is the youngest, but she is neither the shortest nor the tallest.
   b. John is the oldest.
   c. Jeff is younger and taller than Joan, who is shorter than Jane and Jeff.

Problem and Practice

Make a chart to solve each of these problems. *#2* is a real challenge.

1. Three people named Bob, Judy, and Karen have children named Cathy, Martha, and Doug. Martha visits Aunt Judy every summer, but Doug never sees his Uncle Bob or his Aunt Karen. Bob is not related to Cathy. Match each parent with his or her child.

2. Mary, Sam, Harold, and Grace are going to the market to buy fruit. Each one is going to buy his or her favorite fruit. The four fruits they are going to buy are bananas, apples, oranges, and grapes. Use the clues below to figure out the fruit each person will buy. You won't need all of the information to help you solve your problem.

   1. Mary and Grace are best friends.

   2. Mary and Harold don't like orange or yellow fruits.

   3. Grace plays tennis with the boy who likes apples.

   4. Harold is the cousin of the girl who likes bananas.

   5. Harold and Sam go to school together.

Following Directions

Read the passage below. Then follow the directions based on this passage. You will be using your skill in making inferences. Use a separate sheet of paper to do the exercise.

Just as Beth and Bob were crossing the street, a siren sounded and a police car raced around the corner and pulled up at the curb. The police dashed into the bank. Beth and Bob decided to wait to see what was going on. A small crowd gathered, but ten minutes went by before anything else happened. Then the police walked out quickly, got in their car, and drove away.

a. Write your name at the top of the page, about in the center.
b. If the whole event took more than ten minutes, draw a star under your last name. If you can't tell, draw a heart.
c. If Beth and Bob decided to wait before the police went into the bank, draw a heart under the figure you just drew. If they decided after the police went into the bank, draw a circle there. If you can't tell, draw a triangle there.
d. If Beth and Bob were walking away from the bank to start with, draw a square in the bottom left corner. If you can't tell, draw a triangle there.
e. If the bank was being robbed, write **yes** next to the last figure you drew. If you can't tell, write **CT** there.
f. If the police left the bank quickly, put a star in the bottom right corner. If you can't tell, put a heart there.
g. If the police car sounded its siren, write **yes** next to the figure you just drew. If you can't tell, write **CT** there.

Following Directions

Use a separate sheet of paper to follow this set of directions.

To follow these directions you need the following information. Make a chart based on this information before you begin the set of directions.

1. Rob is taller than Dorothy, but Barbara is shorter than Dorothy.
2. The tallest person lives in a yellow house and drives a green car.
3. The shortest person drives a black car and lives in a green house.
4. The person who is neither the tallest nor the shortest drives a blue car and lives in a yellow house.

a. Write the name of the person who lives in a green house in the lower left corner.

b. If more than two people live in yellow houses, write **yellow** near the center of your paper.

c. Write the name of the person who drives a blue car in the lower right corner.

d. If the tallest and shortest people are not both girls, write **girls** along the right edge of the paper.

e. If the person who lives in a green house does not drive a black car, write **black** in the upper right corner.

f. If Rob is taller than the person who drives a blue car, write **blue** along the left edge of the paper.

g. If Dorothy is taller than the person who drives the green car, write **green** along the bottom edge of your paper.

h. Print your name at the top edge of your paper.

Following Directions

Use a separate sheet of paper to follow this set of directions.

a. Write your name on the bottom of the paper about in the center.

b. If all gumps have stripes and Lester is a gump, will Lester have stripes? If so, draw a small circle in the top left corner of the paper. If not, draw a square there.

c. If all hoppers have big legs and Simple has big legs, is Simple a hopper? If so, draw a small triangle in the lower left corner. If we can't be sure, draw a small circle there.

d. If a round table cannot be square, draw a small circle in the upper right corner. Otherwise, draw a small square there.

e. Draw lines connecting the circles on your paper in pairs. Make sure you connect each pair.

f. If you just drew one or two lines, put a star in the lower right corner. If you drew more than two lines, put a heart there.

g. If no swiggles can giggle, and Thump is a swiggle, will he giggle? If he will, draw an arrow from the figure in the top left corner to the figure in the bottom right corner.

Following Directions

Use a separate piece of paper to follow this set of directions.

The YMCA took a busload of junior high students to see a preseason Jets game. At first fourty-two kids signed up for the trip. Three parents volunteered to go along. At the last minute, four kids crossed their names off the list and two added their names to the list. When the bus returned after the game, thirty-eight kids were on board. Some had stayed to visit friends or relatives in the city.

a. Put a dot in the center of your paper.

b. If the trip was run by the YMCA for high school kids, draw a line from the dot to the center of the left edge of your paper. Otherwise, draw a line from the dot to the center of the top of the paper.

c. If more than thirty-nine kids were on the bus going to the game, draw a line from the dot to the top left corner. If fewer than thirty-nine kids were on the bus, draw a line from the dot to the lower left corner.

d. If more than three kids stayed in the city, draw a line from the dot to the lower right corner. If fewer than three kids stayed, draw a line from the dot to the upper right corner.

e. If fewer than six kids changed their minds about whether they were going or not going on the trip, draw an arrow from the dot to the right hand edge of the paper, about in the center. Otherwise, draw an arrow from the dot to the center of the bottom of the page.

f. Print your name along the arrow.